MW00487797

WHAT IS A PEOPLE?

NEW DIRECTIONS IN CRITICAL THEORY

NEW DIRECTIONS IN CRITICAL THEORY

Amy Allen, General Editor

New Directions in Critical Theory presents outstanding classic and contemporary texts in the tradition of critical social theory, broadly construed. The series aims to renew and advance the program of critical social theory, with a particular focus on theorizing contemporary struggles around gender, race, sexuality, class, and globalization and their complex interconnections.

For a complete list of the series see page 165

WHAT IS A PEOPLE?

Alain Badiou, Pierre Bourdieu, Judith Butler,
Georges Didi-Huberman,
Sadri Khiari, and Jacques Rancière

Introduction by Bruno Bosteels
and Conclusion by Kevin Olson

Translated by Jody Gladding

COLUMBIA UNIVERSITY PRESS   NEW YORK

COLUMBIA UNIVERSITY PRESS
Publishers Since 1893
New York   Chichester, West Sussex

cup.columbia.edu
Qu'est-ce qu'un peuple? © 2013 La Fabrique-Éditions
English translation © 2016 Columbia University Press
All rights reserved

Library of Congress Cataloging-in-Publication Data
Names: Badiou, Alain, author.
Title: What is a people? / Alain Badiou, Pierre Bourdieu, Judith Butler,
Georges Didi-Huberman, Sadri Khiari, and Jacques Rancière ;
introduction by Bruno Bosteels and Conclusion by Kevin Olson ;
translated by Jody Gladding.
Other titles: Qu'est-ce qu'un peuple? English
Description: New York : Columbia University Press,
2016. | Series: New directions in critical theory |
Translation of: Qu'est-ce qu'un peuple? |
Includes bibliographical references and index.
Identifiers: LCCN 2015042650 | ISBN 9780231168762
(cloth : alk. paper) | ISBN 9780231541718 (e-book)
Subjects: LCSH: Democracy. | Populism. | Group identity. | People
(Constitutional law) | Political science—Philosophy. | Social
classes—Political aspects. | Nation-state.
Classification: LCC JC423 .Q46513 2016 | DDC 320.56/62—dc23
LC record available at http://lccn.loc.gov/2015042650

Columbia University Press books are printed on permanent
and durable acid-free paper.
This book is printed on paper with recycled content.
Printed in the United States of America

c 10 9 8 7 6 5 4 3 2

Cover design: David Drummond

References to websites (URLs) were accurate at the time of writing.
Neither the author nor Columbia University Press is responsible for URLs
that may have expired or changed since the manuscript was prepared.

CONTENTS

PREFACE

"The child is the interpreter of the people. What am I saying? He is the people itself, in its native truth, before it is deformed, the people without vulgarity, without rudeness, without envy, inspiring neither defiance nor repulsion." Michelet's words can make us smile, but when we speak of popular (language) or of populist (discourse), isn't there a kind of defiance and repulsion there?

The plan for this book grew out of our anxiety at seeing the word "people" hopelessly joined with the group of words like "republic" or "secularism," whose meanings have evolved to serve to maintain the order. Despite their diversity, what the texts brought together here have in common is demonstrating that people remains solidly rooted on the side of emancipation.

WHAT IS A PEOPLE?

THIS PEOPLE WHICH IS NOT ONE

BRUNO BOSTEELS

I

To raise the question "What is a people?" always means at the same time to make some statement, even if only implicitly, about who or what is not a people. The six interventions collected in this slender volume are no exception in this regard: while they all to a greater or lesser extent plead in favor of the people as a political category that is still valid today, they also at the same time draw a negative profile—like a chalk outline at the scene of a crime—of whoever does not constitute a people.

This negative delimitation in turn can be said to take two fundamental forms. On one hand, the category of the people is always overtly or covertly opposed to a series of other categories in political thought that by the same token we are invited to discard, criticize, or overcome. Among such alternative options, we could mention not only nation, state, or civil society but also races, masses, and classes, as well as a whole slew of other terms more typically associated with the disciplines of anthropology, sociology, and so-called group or mass psychology, such as horde, tribe, clan, pack, crowd, commune, or community. To be sure, many of these concepts can and do enter into systematic combinations and historical articulations, most notably around the racialized triad of people, nation, and state so central in the constitution of the modern world-system. But even in such cases where the term becomes part of a larger configuration, any strategic privilege given to the concept of the people immediately causes a chain reaction in the political evaluation of its alternatives. Already the use of the indefinite article in the question "What is *a* people?" invites us to abandon the essentialist presuppositions behind "the" people and opens up the possibility of talking about "peoples" in the plural. This may be linguistically awkward in English but in other languages, such as Spanish, helps draw critical attention to the indigenous presence that continues to resist the colonial framing of the capitalist world-system dominated by the West—with *los pueblos originarios*, for example, constituting key political actors throughout much of Latin America today. On the other hand, no sooner is the term chosen than the people also begins to function as an exclusionary category in its own right, always in need of being internally demarcated from that which is not yet or no longer part thereof and which for this same reason tends to be relegated more or less violently to the pre-political or nonpolitical realm indicated by the pejorative use of terms such as plebs, populace, mob, or rabble.

Whichever way we designate those who are either not the people or other than the people, there is no way of circumnavigating the fact that, both historically and conceptually speaking, this category is constituted on the basis of a necessary exclusion. Specifically, the political logic of the people can be said to operate according to the principle of a constitutive outside in at least a double sense: by choosing the people, or a people, as a privileged term for articulating the sphere of modern politics, contemporary thought inevitably marginalizes or bans from the discussion a number of other terms, while raising the even more troubling issue of how to name and take stock of whoever falls outside of the political realm so designated and often as a result no longer even appears as a "who" deserving of calling itself a subject but ends up being targeted as a mere object of denigration and exploitation. The fundamental decision to be made in this context, however, is whether or not we take this logic of exclusion to be capable of erecting insurmountable obstacles on the path to the continued use of the people as a political category today.

For example, not everyone in today's world of war-and-oil-driven globalization will so readily identify with the seemingly egalitarian and emancipatory invocation of "We, the people," taken up here by Judith Butler as the starting point for a wide-ranging reflection on the self-constitution of political subjects, with a special eye on the new era of protests and uprisings announced in the movements in Tahrir Square in Egypt or Puerta del Sol in Spain. To the contrary, as the opening words of the preamble to the constitution of one country in particular, this expression—at least in English—will strike many as being all too deeply ensnared in the history of the United States of America, from the early days of its independence to its unbridled economic expansionism and military interventionism today. However, does this mean that the subjective self-assertion of any people whatsoever, as the embodiment of a plural "we" emancipating itself from the instituted powers that be, should cease to be prescriptive in general? And should the role of political theory thenceforth be limited to the extreme vigilance with which one points out, stands guard over, and endlessly deconstructs the inevitable hierarchies and exceptions without which no people has ever been capable of constituting itself? Or else, without unduly generalizing one nation's particular history as our universal model, whether that of the United States or France, can the category of the people be salvaged from the combined wreckage of national chauvinism and imperialist expansionism so as to be rescued for genuinely emancipatory purposes? And, in that case, whether it takes place in philosophy or sociology, in political science or the study of language and art, can the work of theory actually contribute to the sharpening of this political potential, rather than shielding itself in the irrefutable radicalism reserved for those rare ones who—standing on the sidelines or tracking down one crisis after the other as so many ambulance chasers—are uniquely capable of seeing through all the blind spots of contemporary politics, whether on the left or on the right?

2

With the possible exception of Pierre Bourdieu's intervention, which was first published more than three decades ago and questions the supposed univocity of the political valence attributed to what sociolinguists define as "popular," the unifying wager behind the texts collected in this volume holds that, far from raising insuperable obstacles that should render the category practically inoperative if not unavailable altogether, the divisions and exclusions that keep the people from ever being one are very much part and parcel of the category's uncanny political efficacy. In spite of certain quibbles between them, no doubt due more to the narcissism of petty differences than to fundamental philosophical disagreements, most contributors to the present volume in this sense could be said to fall in line with the arguments of the late Ernesto Laclau, when in *On Populist Reason* he posits that "the political operation par excellence is always going to be the construction of a 'people.'"[1]

Let us briefly consider, for example, what may well be the founding text for understanding the people as a central political category in the modern age: Jean-Jacques Rousseau's 1762 treatise *The Social Contract*. Rousseau is the eighteenth-century philosopher who, no doubt more than anyone, has given center stage to the coming into being of a people as the modern political act par excellence. For him this means above all to forego the search for the origins of political power in a transcendent source such as the divine right bestowed on a king or dynasty, to whom the people would then have no choice but to devote itself in a blind pledge of allegiance: "Thus, before examining the act whereby a people chooses a king, it would be well to examine the act whereby a people is a people. For since this act is necessarily prior to the other, it is the true foundation of society."[2] Such would be the riddle of the people's foundational act that Rousseau seeks to solve in *The Social Contract*. In reality, despite the apparent tautology of its formulation, this act is riven with paradoxical tensions.

If an act is involved to begin with, then clearly we are not dealing with the evidence of an already given identity. Instead of referring us back to the self-sameness of an essential being, the people is only ever the result of a process of political becoming. More so than a single punctual act, situated at the mythic origin of a people, such a political process involves a prolonged act or series of acts in which a substantial yet immanent transformation takes hold of a collective body. This is the strange magic whereby the whole becomes more than the sum of its parts. Thus, in the distance between the first and the second mention of "a people" in Rousseau's formula, we must assume the occurrence of a true metamorphosis—nothing less than a change in human nature itself, as the young Marx was fond of recalling in his reading of *The Social Contract*: "He who dares to undertake the establishment of a people should feel that he is, so to speak, in a position to change human nature, to transform each individual (who by himself is a perfect and solitary whole), into a part of a larger whole from which this individual receives, in a sense, his life and his being."[3] But this momentous change risks becoming obfuscated behind the use of the copula in "the act by which a people is a people," as if we were dealing not with a momentous transformation but with a seamless tautology between subject and predicate.

The same tension also lies in wait, phrased differently but likewise ready to explode, in the well-known solution offered in *The Social Contract* to the fundamental problem of knowing how to describe what constitutes a people, namely the sealing of an originary compact or contract: "If, therefore, one eliminates from the social compact whatever is not essential to it, one will find that it is reducible to the following terms. Each of us places his person and all his power in common under the supreme direction of the general will; and as one we receive each member as an indivisible part of the whole."[4] The fact that Rousseau couches his solution in these terms, borrowed from the juridical ideology of contract law, only highlights the tension all the more. Indeed, as Louis Althusser has shown in a painstaking analysis of the theoretical contradictions that run through *The Social Contract*, the model of the contract is inadequate and fails to correspond to the terms of the problem for which it is meant as the solution. This is because, even as a philosophical fiction, a contractual exchange supposes a reciprocal relation of give-and-take between two formally equal partners. In Rousseau's formulations, however, a barely disguised contradiction obtains between the many parts ("each of us") that enter into the bargain on one end of the exchange and the indivisible whole ("we as one") that emerges on the opposite end.

Indeed, if, following Althusser's lead, we ask ourselves who are the recipient parties (RPs) in Rousseau's formula of contractual exchange, we can say: "On the one hand they are the individuals taken one by one, and on the other, the 'community.' Hence $RP_1 =$ the individual, and $RP_2 =$ the 'community.'"[5] In *The Social Contract*, though, this second party—the "community" or "collective body" that Rousseau proposes we may also call the "city," the "body politic," or the "republic"—does not even exist before the act of association itself. Here, Rousseau's use of the contract model shows up its inadequacy for describing this originary association, as it cannot conceal the profound imbalance or inequality between the two contracting parties. Althusser describes this inequality as the first *décalage*, or "discrepancy," that begins to tear apart the entire conceptual scaffolding in *The Social Contract*, the one from which, by an inevitable chain effect, a whole series of further "discrepancies" will follow in Rousseau's treatise. Althusser describes the problem as follows:

> In a word, here is the difficulty: in every contract the two Recipient Parties exist prior to and externally to the act of the contract. In Rousseau's Social Contract, only the RP_1 conforms to these conditions. The RP_2 on the contrary, escapes them. It does not exist before the contract for a very good reason: it is itself the *product* of the contract. Hence the paradox of the Social Contract is to bring together two RPs, one of which exists both prior to and externally to the contract, while the other does not, since it is the product of the contract itself, or better: its object, its end.[6]

Rousseau, who certainly cannot be said to have been unaware of this problem, nevertheless constantly tries to repress the force of its paradoxical tension. We already saw one example of this effort at denial and concealment in the original formulation of "the act by which a people is a people," with its obfuscating use of the copula. In another formulation from *The Social Contract* the attempt to conceal the discrepancy between the two contracting parties is both partially avowed, by admitting to a certain play on words with a fictive "as it were," and promptly disavowed so as to reaffirm the relation of reciprocity in terms of the apparent self-sameness of an "individual contracting with himself," as when Rousseau writes: "This formula shows that the act of association includes a reciprocal commitment between the public and private individuals, and that *each individual, contracting, as it were, with himself* finds himself under a twofold commitment: namely as a member of the sovereign to private individuals, and as a member of the state toward the sovereign."[7] And in his *Émile*, too, Rousseau suggests that the singularity of his notion of the contract lies in the fact that we would be dealing with a relation of such near-perfect exchangeability that the two contracting parties would seem to be one and the same. Only now he gives this party directly the name of the people and then repeats this name on both sides of the contractual exchange: "The nature of the social pact is private and peculiar to itself, in that *the people only contracts with itself.*"[8] Here, the philosophical fiction of a contract with oneself comes to substitute for the political transformation that must be assumed to take place in the gap between two fundamentally different terms.

Whether he chooses to generalize and reduplicate the name of the first or the second partner in his model of the social contract, Rousseau in each case is at pains to reach a formulation in which the object or end of the political act par excellence would already coincide with the very subject of this same act. Thus, the circle may appear to be squared, but only at the cost of leaving the subject itself split in a twofold commitment—fidelity both to the sovereign body of the new collective and to each of its individual members—that is immediately repressed and covered up by the repetition of a single name.

As Althusser further suggests, in Rousseau's hesitation between the individual and the people as the privileged name for this entity that would be contracting with itself, we can also locate the source for the difference in orientation between two major trends in later political philosophy, signaled by the respective names of Kant and Hegel:

> In the first case, the contract is an anticipation of a theory of Morality, whose voice can be heard in certain already Kantian formulations (liberty as obedience to the law one has given oneself, etc.). In the second case, the contract is an anticipation of a theory of the Nation as a totality, a moment of the Objective Spirit which reveals its basic determinations on a number of occasions

(the historical conditions of possibility of the contract, the theory of manners and morals, of religion, etc.). In both cases the philosophical object Social Contract is relieved of its primordial function. Neither Kantian Morality nor the Hegelian Nation are constituted by a "contract." Besides, is it not enough to *read* Rousseau closely to see that his Contract is not a contract?[9]

Finally, if we consider how the political subject that emerges from Rousseau's treatise must split its commitment between its role as a private individual and its role as a member of the new body politic, we might add to Althusser's suggestion that this discrepancy in *The Social Contract* also announces the Marxist critique of the limits of modern politics. For instance, Marx will make a different formulation of the same discrepancy, namely the split between "man" and "citizen" in the "Declaration of the Rights of Man and of the Citizen," into the pivot around which he organizes his critique of merely "political emancipation" as opposed to "human emancipation" in "On the Jewish Question."[10] Kant, Hegel, and Marx's future paths thus would already be contained conceptually in the hollow spaces carved out in *The Social Contract*.

3

We need not follow Althusser's entire analysis in detail to draw the conclusion that Rousseau's answer to the question "What is a people?"—an answer that by the same token lays the ground for many of the fundamental orientations in political philosophy that are still with us today—reveals the inescapable play of difference at the heart of this fundamental category of modern politics. However, the more important question concerns once again what is to be done with this revelation.

For the canonical Althusser, the one who devoted his 1965–66 seminar to *The Social Contract* right after having made a major name for himself with the publication in 1965 of both his own collection of signature essays in *For Marx* and the collective volume *Reading Capital*, the answer to this question demands a form of symptomatic reading that is not unlike the exercise of deconstruction that around the same time his younger colleague Jacques Derrida was inaugurating—incidentally also on the basis of some of Rousseau's writings. What is different from the orientation of the author of *Of Grammatology* is that for Althusser the task of symptomatic reading in the end still amounts to a form of ideology critique. His analysis of the textual discrepancies and theoretical differences that from beginning to end traverse *The Social Contract* thus concludes by pinpointing the place where Rousseau himself finally hesitates between a flight forward into sheer ideology (with a theory of morals, education, and civil religion centered on the protection of the concept of liberty) and a regression or flight backward into the economy (with the factual recognition of the realities of the class struggle in the form of different group, class, or party interests whose existence nevertheless cannot be allowed to undermine the general will).

Rousseau, at the very moment when in defense of the will of the people he seeks to silence or suppress all groups, orders, factions, classes, parties, and so on, cannot help but accept their existence: "The true Social Contract, now a 'legitimate' one, thus finds at the end of the displacement of its concepts the very same realities whose existence and implacable logic had been described in the *Discourse on Inequality*."[11] The tensions in Rousseau's treatise at this point are no longer purely theoretical but concern the discrepant relation of theory itself with respect to the real; they thus become an eminently practical affair. "The solution to the existing 'theoretical difficulties' is entrusted to practice. It is a question of managing to suppress, in the reality which can no longer be avoided, the social groups and their effects: the existence of orders, of social classes, of political and ideological parties and of their effects," Althusser concludes. "As we are now in reality, and can only turn round and round in it (ideology-economy-ideology, etc.), there is no further flight possible in reality itself. End of the Discrepancy."[12] The only further option for Rousseau, at least according to Althusser, is to transfer the impossible theoretical solution to the realm of literature as an alternative to theory, in the writing of such masterpieces as *La Nouvelle Héloïse* and the *Confessions*, whereas presumably for the author of *For Marx* and *Reading Capital* himself, the only valid option is to refuse the temptations of both literature and ideology by offering a scientific investigation into the positivities of the class struggle following the laws of motion of capital described by Marx.

In stark contrast to this form of ideology critique performed in the name of Marxism as the science of history, for Althusser's better-known students, many of whom were able to start out on their own only after breaking with the stifling authority of their former teacher in the way Jacques Rancière did in 1974 with *Althusser's Lesson* and Alain Badiou two years later in *Of Ideology*, what otherwise appears to be the effect of a theoretical inconsistency or shortcoming, due to the inevitable play of difference within the text of modern political theory, is the belated attempt to give a name to the real efficacy of actual politics. Thus, contrary even to Marx's critical reading of the gap between "man" and "citizen," the distance of the people from itself—the internal difference that keeps it from ever being one—is not an impediment but rather the very key to unlock its true political effectiveness. "For politics, the fact that the people are internally divided is not, actually, a scandal to be deplored. It is the primary condition of the exercise of politics," Rancière proposes in his most systematic book on the subject, *Disagreement: Philosophy and Politics*. He goes on to explain:

> There is politics from the moment there exists the sphere of appearance of a subject, *the people*, whose particular attribute is to be different from itself, internally divided. So, from the political point of view, the inscriptions of equality that figure in the Declaration

of the Rights of Man or the preambles to the Codes and Constitutions, those that symbolize such and such an institution or are engraved on the pediments of their edifices, are not "forms" belied by their contents or "appearances" made to conceal reality. They are an effective mode of appearance of the people, the minimum of equality that is inscribed in the field of common experience. The problem is not to accentuate the difference between this existing equality and all that belies it. It is not to contradict appearances but, on the contrary, to confirm them. Wherever the part of those who have no part is inscribed, however fragile and fleeting these inscriptions may be, a sphere of appearance of the *demos* is created, an element of the *kratos*, the power of the people, exists. The problem is to extend the sphere of this appearance, to maximize this potential.[13]

For Rancière, moreover, the same reasoning about the political efficacy of what from a logical point of view may appear to be sheer paralogisms, theoretical inconsistencies, or speculative impasses holds true not only for "people" but also for many other *gros mots* in our political lexicon—including "worker" and "proletarian" that would have been the dominant terms in the heyday of Marxism. This is why in the eyes of the author of *Proletarian Nights* there is nothing obsolete about continuing to insist on such terms, even long after Marxism has entered into a definitive crisis. As Rancière also argues in the presentation of *Staging the People: The Proletarian and His Double*, a collection of writings for the most part published between the late 1970s and early 1980s in the journal *Les Révoltes Logiques*: "To insist on the overly broad words of people, worker, and proletarian is to insist on their inherent difference, on the space of dissenting invention that this difference offers."[14] Here, instead of functioning as a form of antipolitical leverage that allows the superior intellects of deconstructive theory to unmask the ideological illusions of autonomy and self-presence at work in all modern politics, the difference or discrepancy inherent in categories such as the people is precisely what offers a place for political inventiveness—a heterotopian space or stage where the "play" that such words give, like a door that stands ajar or a window that cannot be shut tight, opens itself up to productive displacements and transformations.

Another way of stating this difference in approach between Althusser and some of his ex-students whose work is featured in the present collection would require that we interpret "play" not just in the linguistic or mechanical but also in a theatrical sense. This interpretation in turn presupposes that we abandon the quintessentially philosophical oppositions between ideas and reality, between form and content, or between appearance and essence. "There is not, on the one hand, the ideal people of the founding texts and, on the other, the real people of the workshops and poor neighborhoods" but only a mixed scene to be staged and interpreted in between: "And so it is no longer a matter of interpreting the difference between one people and another according to some kind of symptomatology. It is a matter of interpreting, in the theatrical sense of the word, the gap between a place where the *demos* exists and a place where it does not, where there are only populations, individuals, employers and employees, heads of households and spouses, and so on."[15] To adopt a theatrical interpretation of the staging of the people in politics, moreover, in retrospect gives a whole new meaning to the fact that at the heart of *For Marx* we already find a text dedicated to the theater, in which Althusser makes the rather condescending claim that being on the side of the people always involves playing at being the people: "One makes oneself 'one of the people' by flirtatiously being above its own methods; that is why it is essential to play at being (not being) the people that one forces the people to be, the people of popular 'myth,' people with a flavor of melodrama. This melodrama is not worthy of the stage (the real, theatrical stage). It is savored in small sips in the cabaret."[16] For someone like Rancière, who decided to collect many of his best writings under the title *Les Scènes du peuple*, or for the seasoned playwright that Badiou also is, this provocative claim by no means should be read as an all-out condemnation of the politics of the people. On the contrary, if the people can only ever be staged, this is because there exists no necessary or natural connection between a particular actor or agent and its assigned role in history. Hence the need for what Laclau, making a similar argument from within a slightly different tradition, calls a contingent hegemonic articulation: "This relationship by which a sector takes up tasks that are not its own is what the Russian social-democrats called *hegemony*."[17] In fact, had the role of certain actors been wholly predetermined and transparently inscribed in the forward march of history, there would be no need for a political articulation to begin with.

Between the social category of the working class and the political operator of the proletariat, for instance, there exists no essential connection or linear relation of transitivity according to Badiou, Laclau, or Rancière. Instead, in every case such a connection must be interpreted, staged, and acted out—Butler might say performed— according to the singular demands of the situation at hand. Therein lies precisely the crux of any political action. "Politics consists in interpreting this relationship, which means first setting it up as theater, inventing the argument, in the double logical and dramatic sense of the term," in a way that differs both from classical theories of sovereignty based on the people's self-alienation, as in Hobbes or Rousseau, and from their scientific critique in the name of the social positivity and consciousness of the working class, as in Marx: "This invention is neither the feat of the sovereign people and its 'representatives' nor the feat of the nonpeople/people of labor and their sudden 'awareness' or *prise de conscience*."[18] Instead, Rancière prefers to speak in terms of a "third people," incidentally using the same French expression, *le tiers peuple*, that appears in the title of Sadri Khiari's contribution to the present volume.

In sum, as both Georges Didi-Huberman and Sadri Khiari also insist in nearly identical terms, *the* people as one and indivisible simply does not exist. Instead, to use the words of Rancière, there are always *several peoples* in the plural, none of which is so stable and straightforward as to correspond, for example, to the simplified schemes of workerism, economism, or orthodox Marxism. This is why Rancière, in *Staging the People*, affirms the intimate link between the people's theater, including its inevitable flavor of melodrama, and the people *as* theater, with history as its stage: "The people's theater, like the people's revolution, has always had several peoples, equally irreducible to the simplicity of the Marxist proletarian, the trade unionist, or the plebs that intellectual fashion formerly celebrated."[19]

Here we are asked to acknowledge the extent to which the evaluation of keywords such as people, proletariat, or plebs—we might add the notion of the multitude, favored by authors such as Antonio Negri and Michael Hardt—is always open to changing historical trends. Clearly the meaning of these terms cannot be ascertained once and for all. But their rise to fame, or alternatively their fall from grace, far from being the direct effect of this or that thinker's otherwise admirable efforts at theoretical systematicity, should be interpreted as the specific result of social, material, and political developments. Thus the revalorization of the category of the people, in which the present volume marks a significant moment, can be said to be due to passing intellectual fashions only if the latter in turn are seen as ways of fighting out the meaning of changing historical circumstances. In particular, the timing of the interventions that follow coincides with a twofold phenomenon: not only the rise of various left-wing populisms in Latin America, from Hugo Chávez in Venezuela to Evo Morales in Bolivia, but also, and above all, the declining belief in the proletariat's capacity for revolutionary politics, symptomatic of the crisis of orthodox Marxism.

However, aside from a paradigm shift from the proletariat to the people, which every day risks pushing more and more post-Marxists into the open arms of neo-populists, there also exists a very different tradition in thinking of the people that would appear to be almost completely absent from the present volume and is only indirectly alluded to in the language of the *Volk*. The latter, in fact, is not just the common German word for "people," it arguably also serves as an untranslatable code word to refer to the closed communitarian understanding of the *Volksgemeinschaft* in Nazi Germany. Philosophically, this tradition no doubt finds its most troubling expression in the work of Martin Heidegger, whose National-Socialist commitment—no matter how brief it may have been in the official record—still has not ceased provoking polemical demarcations and painstaking explanations from his critics. Among post-Heideggerian thinkers in France, such as Philippe Lacoue-Labarthe, Jean-Luc Nancy, and Maurice Blanchot, whose work for the same reason perhaps should have been represented more fully in the present volume than what a brief mention in Didi-Huberman's essay alone can do justice to, we can thus situate a radical effort at deconstructing the twin categories of the people as *Volk* and the community as *Gemeinschaft*.

Let us recall how in an important section of his 1927 *Being and Time* (§74, "The Essential Constitution of Historicity"), Heidegger had tried to project the authentic existence of the human being qua *Da-sein*, or "being-there," onto the sphere of world history. For the thinker from Todtnauberg, authenticity at the level of history requires a decisive readiness to retrieve the existential possibilities handed down from tradition and appropriate them as formative of one's own fate: not as the inherited legacy of what is merely past and bygone but as the possibility of a genuine choice that comes to existence out of the future. Such an anticipatory resoluteness, by which famously "*Da-sein* may choose its heroes," is what Heidegger sees as grounding a community or a people's innermost "destiny":

With this term, we designate the occurrence of the community, of a people. Destiny is not composed of individual fates, nor can being-with-one-another be conceived of as the mutual occurrence of several subjects. These fates are already guided beforehand in being-with-one-another in the same world and in the resoluteness for definite possibilities. In communication and in battle the power of destiny first becomes free. The fateful destiny of *Da-sein* in and with its "generation" constitutes the complete, authentic occurrence of *Da-sein*.[20]

Admittedly, all these terms—resoluteness, authenticity, choice, decision, fate, freedom, and so on—may seem part of a vocabulary that is all too susceptible to psychological and moral-anthropological interpretations, to the point where Heidegger himself came to feel the need, after the so-called *Kehre* or "turn" in his thinking, to move away from the emphasis on the authentic human being to the event of being as such. And yet, even while pointing out the danger of misinterpreting *Being and Time* in an overly existentialist or humanist direction, in his later writings this same thinker does not stop pondering what constitutes a people as a crucial part of the proposed turn toward being. Thus, in his private musings from 1936 to 1938, published posthumously under the title *Contributions to Philosophy (Of the Event)*, for example, Heidegger explicitly asks the very same questions that form the starting point for the interventions in the present volume: "How does a people become a people? Does a people become only that which it *is*? If so, then what *is* it? How can we know: (1) What a people in general is? (2) What this or that people is? (3) What we ourselves are?"[21]

In other words, Heidegger's emphasis may have shifted from the human being's resolute decision to its meditative rootedness in being as such, but even his later thinking remains inseparable from the mission to give shape to a people endowed with the world-historical task of preparing those essential occurrences that alone might be able to change the nihilist course of the West, for example, by giving us a glimpse of the coming of the last God. "The selfhood of the human being—of the historical human being as the selfhood of a people—is a realm of occurrences, a realm in which human beings are appropriated to themselves only if they themselves reach the open time-space wherein an appropriation can occur," Heidegger still muses in *Contributions to Philosophy*. "The most proper 'being' of humans is therefore grounded in a belonging to the truth of being as such, and this is so, again, because the essence of being as such, not the essence of the human being, contains in itself a call to humans, as a call destining them to history."[22] Even Lacoue-Labarthe, who in his lifelong investigation into the matter never accepted the charge of Heidegger's anti-Semitism and passed away before the publication of the notorious *Black Notebooks* might have changed his mind, had to admit that the notion of a turn in the fundamental orientation of Heidegger's thinking was more wish-fulfilling fantasy than reality on the part of the German thinker. "Between 1933 and 1967, the tone has obviously changed: the pathos of meditation has been substituted for the pathos of resolution and there is no call for a national revolution. . . . Yet the 'message' is the same and the—now veiled—injunction is identical: the leap called for (breach and leap into the origin) is now called 'step back,' but it is still the destiny of Western Europe that is at stake in it," Lacoue-Labarthe concludes in *Heidegger, Art, and Politics: The Fiction of the Political*. "It is clear, then, that Heidegger never ceased to connect the possibility of History (historiality) with the possibility of a people or of the people. Which always meant conjointly, as we know, with the possibility of an art (a *Dichtung*), a language and a myth (a *Sage*, i.e., a relation with the gods)."[23]

For those thinkers who nonetheless are prepared to stay within a certain Heideggerian mind-set in order to offer their critique, the lesson that we are expected to draw from this line of thinking holds that the deconstruction of metaphysics must be pushed to the limit so as to tackle the hegemonic desire of and for philosophy still present in Heidegger's own thought in its disastrous affiliation with Nazism. Thus a radical critique not only of Heidegger's personal commitments but also of all hitherto existing forms of political subjectivization, whether they go by the name of the people or not, should serve as a constant reminder to renounce the misguided hopes placed in philosophy's ability to provide spiritual guidance or leadership to the political guide or leader. "The commitment of 1933 is founded upon the idea of an hegemony of the spiritual and the philosophical over political hegemony itself (this is the theme of a *Führung* of the *Führung* or of the *Führer*) which leads us back at least to the Platonic *basileía*," but which in Heidegger's case becomes compatible with Nazism through the supporting reference to the rootedness of a particular people, i.e., the German *Volk.* "In Heideggerian terms, the question is, as I have indicated, the following: why is historial *Dasein* determined as the *Dasein* of a *people?*" asks Lacoue-Labarthe. "In more banally political terms, we may transcribe this question as follows: why was Heidegger committed to the idea of a national Revolution and why did he never repudiate that commitment?"[24]

Faced with the legacy of Heidegger's undeniable political compromises, thinkers such as Lacoue-Labarthe and Nancy call for an interruption of the general logic according to which philosophy would be able to lead the way to the resolute appropriation of an authentic destiny, whether by a solitary individual or a historic people. After Auschwitz, all such fictive "putting to work" of the people or of the community must be broken off, emptied out, and rendered inoperative. And if the ultimate workability of politics is what philosophy has always desired, from as early as Plato to as late as Heidegger, then perhaps we should in all modesty be without the desire for philosophy: "A very obscure imperative, beyond or beneath the mere refusal of what is dominant, commands that we let philosophy collapse within ourselves and that we open ourselves up to that diminishing, that exhaustion of philosophy, today. We must no longer have the desire to philosophize."[25] From a post-Heideggerian point of view, in other words, the issue is not to decide between the people, the proletariat, or any other privileged name for the political subject today but instead to come to grips with the notion that the will to subjectivity in general is nothing but the modern culmination of Western metaphysics.

To understand the texts that follow, by contrast, we have to assume that the category of the people *already* has undergone a painstaking internal critique or deconstruction. As I have tried to show via one line of thinking that links Rousseau to some of Althusser's best-known disciples, this also means that there is no people before the act by which a people becomes a people in the first place; and, even afterward, the people are never one or homogeneous but many and internally divided. In sum, far from constituting a stable identity derived from a preordained essence that would have been racially, ethnically, linguistically, culturally, or ontologically definable, "people" here serves as a name—one name among others—for the political process that produces its own subject, while reminding us that without an element of subjectivization there can be no politics.

1

TWENTY-FOUR NOTES ON THE USES OF THE WORD "PEOPLE"

ALAIN BADIOU

I

Even if we can only nod, time and again, to the "we are here by the will of the people" of the nascent French Revolution, we must acknowledge that "people," by itself, is not in the least a progressive noun. When Mélanchon's posters proclaim "a place for the people!" it is only unreadable rhetoric today. Likewise we must acknowledge that neither is "people" a fascist term, even if the Nazi uses of the word *Volk* seem inclined in that direction. When Marine Le Pen's "populism" is denounced almost everywhere, this only adds to the confusion. The truth is that "people" is now a neutral term, like so many others in the political lexicon. Everything is a matter of context. Thus we will have to examine it a bit more closely.

2

The adjective "popular" is more connotative, more active. We have only to look at what was meant by expressions like "popular committee," "popular movement," "popular tribunal," "popular front," "popular power," and, even on the state level, "popular democracy," to say nothing of "popular liberation army," to observe that the adjective aims at politicizing the noun, at conferring upon it an aura that combines the breaking off of oppression and the light of a new collective life. Of course if a singer or a politician is "popular," it is only a statistical fact without real value. But not if a movement or an insurrection is so classified exactly like such episodes in areas of history where it was a question of emancipation.

3

On the other hand, we distrust the word "people" when it is accompanied by an adjective, especially an adjective of identity or nationality.

4

We know of course that there was nothing legitimate or politically positive about the "heroic war of liberation of the Vietnamese people." It seems that "liberation" in the context of colonial oppression, indeed even in the context of an intolerable foreign invasion, confers upon "people"—accompanied by an adjective that characterizes said people— an undeniable liberating touch. And all the more so when the imperial colonial camp would prefer to speak of "tribes" or "ethnic groups," if not "races" and "savages." The word "people" was only suitable for the conquering powers, elated by the conquest itself: "the French people," "the English people," yes. . . . But the Algerian people, the Vietnamese people? No! And even today for the Israeli government, "the Palestinian

people"? An even louder no. The period of the wars of national liberation sanctified "national adjective + people," by establishing the right—
often at the cost of armed struggle—to the word "people" for those to
whom the colonizers refused its use, considering only themselves to be
"true" peoples.

5

But beyond the violent process of liberation, beyond the movement
to appropriate a forbidden word, of what value is "national adjective
+ people"? Not much, let's admit it. And especially now. Because now
is the time when the truth of one of Marx's powerful maxims asserts
itself, a sentence as forgotten as it is forceful, even though it was crucial in the eyes of its author: "The workers have no country." This is even
more true because although they have always been nomads—since they
had to uproot themselves from the land and rural poverty to be enlisted
into capitalism's workshops—workers are more nomadic now than ever.
No longer are they just moving from the country to the city but from
Africa and Asia to Europe and America, even from Cameroon to Shang-
hai or from the Philippines to Brazil. Thus to what "national adjective +
people" do they belong? Much more than when Marx, that great prophet
of the future of the classes, was forming the First International, now is
the time when the workers are the living body of internationalism, the
only territory where something like a "proletariat" can exist, "proletariat"
understood here as the subjectivized body of communism.

6

We must abandon to their reactionary fate expressions like "the French
people" and other phrases in which "people" is saddled with an identity. Where "the French people" in reality means nothing more than

"the inert mass of those upon whom the state has conferred the right to call themselves French." We will accept this yoking only in cases where that identity is in reality a political process under way, as with "the Algerian people" during the French war in Algeria, or the "Chinese people" when the expression is pronounced from the communist base of Yan'an. And in these cases we should note that "adjective + people" derives its reality only in violent opposition to another "adjective + people," the one with a colonial army breathing down its neck that claims to refuse insurgents any right to the word "people," or the army of a reactionary state that desires the extermination of "anti-national" rebels.

7

Thus "adjective + people" is either an inert category of the state (like "French people" today from the mouths of politicians on both sides) or a category of wars and political processes associated with situations of so-called national liberation.

8

In parliamentary democracies in particular, the "people" has in fact become a category of the right of state. Through the political sham of the vote, the "people," composed of a collection of human atoms, confers the fiction of legitimacy on the elected. This is the "sovereignty of the people," or more exactly the sovereignty of the "French people." If for Rousseau sovereignty still meant a live and effective popular assembly—let us recall that Rousseau considered English parliamentary government to be a sham—it is clear today that such sovereignty, with its multiplicity of inert and fragmented opinions, constitutes no true political subject. As legal referent for the representative process, the "people" means only that the state can and must persist in its being.

9

"What being?" we will ask. And so without going into detail here we will propose that our states do not in the least derive their reality from the vote but rather from an insurmountable allegiance to the necessities of capitalism and the antipopular measures (let us stress in passing the undoubtedly strained values that derive from the adjective "popular") that those necessities constantly require. And this is happening more and more overtly, more and more shamelessly. And that is how our "democratic" governments make the people, whom they claim to represent, into a substance we may call *capitalized*. If you don't believe it, if like Saint Thomas you believe only in what you can see, look at Hollande.

10

But can't the "people" be a reality that underlies the progressive virtue of the adjective "popular"? Isn't a "popular assembly" a kind of representation of the "people" in a different sense than the closed, state-controlled one masked by adjectives of nationality and the "democratic" legalization of sovereignty?

11

Let us return to the example of the wars of national liberation. In this context, "the Vietnamese people" means in effect the existence of a people just as it was refused status as referent for a nation, which can itself only exist on the global scene insofar as it is granted a state. Thus it is *in the retrospective effect of the nonexistence of a state* that the "people" can be part of the naming of a political process and thus become a political category. As soon as the state in question is formed, regulated, and enrolled in the "international community," the people it claims as its authority ceases to be a political subject. It becomes a passive mass that the state configures, universally, no matter what the form of the state.

12

But within this passive mass, can't "people" designate something singular? If we consider, for example, the great strikes in France during the Occupation in June 1936 or in May 1968, don't we have to say that a people—a "working people"—emerged there as a kind of immanent exception to the constitutional inertia designated by the expression "the French people"? Yes, we can, we must say it. And as early as Spartacus and his rebellious companions, or Toussaint Louverture and his friends both black and white, we must say that in ancient Rome or on the colonial island of Haiti, they configured a true people.

13

Even the dangerous inertia of the word "people" modified by a national adjective can, despite the contradiction, be subverted by pressure from within this national and lawful "people." What did those who occupied Tahrir Square in Egypt at the height of the "Arab Spring" mean when they asserted, "We are the Egyptian people"? That their movement, their own unity, their slogans configure an Egyptian people free from its established national inertia, an Egyptian people with the right to actively claim the national adjective, *because the nation of which they speak is yet to come.* Because it only exists in the dynamic form of a vast political movement. Because, in the face of that movement, the state that claims to represent Egypt is illegitimate and must disappear.

14

From which we see that "people" here takes on a meaning that implies the disappearance of the existing state. And, beyond that, the disappearance of state itself, from the moment that political decisions are in the hands of a new people assembled on a square, assembled *right here*. What is affirmed in vast popular movements is always the latent necessity of what Marx made the supreme objective of all revolutionary politics: the demise of the state.

15

Let us note that in all these cases, in the place of the electoral process's majority *representation*, which shapes the state-controlled inertia of the people through the legal means of state legitimacy, and also in the place of *submission*, always half consensual and half forced, to a despotic authority, we have a minority *detachment* that activates the word "people" according to an unprecedented political orientation. The "people" can once again designate—in a context completely different from the one of struggles for national liberation—the subject of a political process. But it is always in the form of a minority that *declares* not that it *represents* the people but that it *is* the people as it destroys its own inertia and makes itself the body of the political precedent.

16

Let us note that this minority detachment can only enforce its declaration ("we are the people, the true people") insofar as, beyond its own strength, beyond the small numbers that make it the body of the political precedent, it is constantly *tied* to a living popular mass by a thousand channels and actions. Speaking of that specific and specialized detachment that called itself "the Communist Party" in the last century, Mao Zedong indicated that his legitimacy was at every moment suspended from what he called the "mass liaison," which was in his eyes the alpha and omega of the possible *reality* of a politics. Let us say that the immanent exception that is the people in the sense of an active detachment only supports its claim of being the provisional body of the true people in a lasting way by validating that claim at any moment within the wide masses, by deploying its activity in the direction of those whom the inert people, subject to its configuration by the state, keeps forever at a distance from their political capacity.

17

But isn't there also the "people" in the sense that, even without ever activating an assembled detachment, is nevertheless not truly included in the contingent of "the sovereign people" as constituted by the state? We will answer "yes." It makes sense to speak of "the people's people" as they are *what the official people, in the guise of the state, regards as nonexistent.* Here we arrive at the margins of objectivity, the social, economic, and state margins. For centuries the "nonexistent" mass was the mass of poor peasants, and the existent society properly speaking, as deemed by the state, consisted of a mix of hereditary aristocracy and the nouveaux riches. Today in the societies that grant themselves the title of "advanced" societies or "democracies," the central core of the nonexistent mass is composed of newly arrived workers (those called "immigrants"). Around them is a loose composite of provisional workers, the underemployed, displaced intellectuals, and the entirety of exiled, segregated youth on the peripheries of large cities. It is legitimate to speak of the "people" with regard to this ensemble, insofar as, in the eyes of the state, it has no right to the consideration the official people enjoys.

Let us remark that in our societies, the official people is given the very strange name of the "middle class." As if what is "middle" could be admirable. . . . That is because the dominant ideology of our societies is Aristotelian. Counter to the obvious aristocratism of Plato, Aristotle established the excellence of what cleaves to the golden mean. That is the grounds for the creation of a significant middle class as the necessary medium for a democratic-style constitution. Today when the official propaganda newspapers (that is to say, nearly all the newspapers) rejoice over the growth of the Chinese middle class—they have counted, feverishly . . . —to five hundred million people, consumers of new products who want to be left in peace, they are the unknowing followers of Aristotle. Their conclusion is the same as his: in China, a democracy—the happy medium . . . —is in sight, for which the "people" is the satisfied ensemble of the middle class that constitutes the masses so that the power of the capitalist oligarchy can be considered democratically legitimate.

19

The middle class is the "people" of capitalist oligarchies.

20

From this perspective, the Malian, Chinese, Moroccan, Congolese, or Tamil who is refused legal status, to whom papers are denied, is the emblem of the people in that he is and can only be what is rescued of the word "people" from the false people composed of those who form a consensus around the oligarchy. Moreover, that is why the process of political organization around the issue of papers, and more generally around the issues related to the newest arrivals among workers, is central to all progressive politics today; it can configure the new people as it is constituted on the margins of the official people in order to rescue for it the word "people" as a political word.

21

Thus we have two negative senses of the word "people." The first and most obvious is the one saddled with a closed—and always fictive—racial or national identity. The historical existence of this type of "people" requires the construction of a despotic state, which brings its founding fiction violently into existence. The second, more subtle one, though on a large scale even more harmful—because of its adaptability and the consensus that it fosters—is the one that subordinates the recognition of a "people" to a state that is assumed to be legitimate and beneficent by the sole fact that it organizes when possible the growth, and in any case the persistence, of a middle class, free to consume the empty products that capitalism force-feeds it and free as well to say what it wants, provided that this free speech has no effect whatsoever on the general mechanism.

22

And finally we have two positive senses of the word "people." The first is the constitution of a people in pursuit of its historical existence, insofar as that aim is denied by colonial and imperial domination or by the domination of an invader. Thus the "people" exists according to the future perfect of a nonexistent state. The second is the existence of a people who declares itself as such, beginning from its central core, which is precisely what the official state excludes from its supposedly legitimate "people." Such a people asserts its existence politically in the strategic aim of abolishing the existing state.

23

The "people" is therefore a political category, either leading up to the existence of a desired state denied existence by some power or in the aftermath of an established state of which a new people, both interior and exterior to the official people, requires its demise.

24

The word "people" has a positive sense only with regard to the possible nonexistence of the state. Either the forbidden state whose creation is desired. Or the official state whose disappearance is desired. The "people" is a word that takes all its value either, in transitory forms, from the wars of national liberation or, in definitive forms, from communist politics.

2

YOU SAID "POPULAR"?

PIERRE BOURDIEU

POPULAR. *Adj.* (*Populeir*, XIIᵉ; lat. *popularis*). 1: What belongs to the people, emanates from the people. *Popular government.* *"The Greek politics that lived in the popular government"* (Montesquieu). See Democratic. *Popular democracies. Popular demonstration, insurrection. Popular front:* the union of leftist powers (communists, socialists, etc.). *The popular masses.* 2: Belonging to the people. *Popular belief, traditions. Popular good sense.* — *Ling.* What is created and used by the people and rarely used among the bourgeoisie and cultivated classes. *Popular word, expression. Popular Latin. Popular expression, locution, turn of phrase.* For the use of the people (and emanating from them or not). *Popular novel, show. Popular songs. Popular art* (See Folklore). — (*Individuals*) Who address themselves to the people. *"You must not be successful as a popular speaker"* (Maurois). Who is recruited among the people, what the people frequent. *Popular circles, classes. "They found a new formula: to work for a downright popular clientele"* (Romains). *Popular origins.* See Plebeian. *Popular balls. Popular soups.* 3: (1559) What pleases the people, in the greatest number. *Henri IV was a popular king. Popular measure. "Hoffmann is popular in France, more popular than in Germany"* (Gautier). 4: Noun (Vx). *The popular,* the people. ANT. (of 3:) *Unpopular.*

—*Le Petit Robert* (1979)

The idioms that include the magic epithet "popular" are protected from scrutiny by the fact that all critical analysis of a notion touching closely or distantly on the "people" is subject immediately to being identified as a symbolic aggression against the reality so designated—and thus immediately denounced by all those whose duty it is to defend the cause of the "people" and to thus ensure themselves the profits that defending "good causes," especially in favorable circumstances, can also procure.[1] That is the case with the notion of "popular language," which, in the manner of all expressions in the same family ("popular culture," "popular art," "popular religion," and so on) is only defined relationally, as is the whole of what is excluded from legitimate language by, among other things, the durable action of inculcation and imposition matched with sanctions exercised by the school system.

As slang or "nonconventional French" dictionaries clearly reveal, the so-called popular lexicon is nothing other than the whole of the words that are excluded from the dictionaries of legitimate language or that only appear there accompanied by negative "usage marks": *fam.*, familiar, "that is to say commonly used in ordinary spoken language and in casual written language"; *pop.*, popular, "that is to say commonly used among the urban popular or working classes but reproved or avoided by the cultivated bourgeoisie."[2] In order to define with utmost rigor this "popular" or "nonconventional" language, better referred to as *pop.* henceforth, lest we forget the social conditions of its production, we must thus specify what is meant by the expression "popular or working classes" and what is to be understood by "commonly used."

Like the variable geometry concepts of the "popular classes," the "people," or the "workers," which owe their political virtues to the fact that their referents can be expanded as desired—in election periods for example—to include rural populations, managerial staff, and small business owners or, on the contrary, restricted to include just industrial workers or even just steelworkers (and their appointed representatives), the notion of "popular or working classes," with its indeterminate extension, owes its trickster virtues, in scholarly production, to the fact that anyone can, as in a projective test, unconsciously manipulate that extension to adjust it to one's own interests, prejudices, or social fantasies. That is why, when it is a matter of designating the speakers of the "popular language," everyone agrees to consider the "lowlife," given the idea that the "toughs" play a determinant role in the production and circulation of slang, resolutely excluded from legitimate dictionaries. We must be sure to include as well the indigenous workers of urban stock that the word "popular" almost automatically evokes whereas rural workers will automatically be excluded with little more justification (no doubt because they are known to be destined for the usage mark of *region.*, regional). But the question will not even arise—and this is one of the most precious functions of these catchall notions—if the small business owners must be excluded or not, especially the café owners whom the populist imagination will undoubtedly exclude, whereas, for the culture as for the language, they are indisputably closer to the workers than the middle-level management and employees. And it is certain in any case that the fantasy, nourished more on Marcel Carné films than on observation, that most often directs the folklorist recollection of nostalgic renegades toward the "purest" of the most "authentic" representatives of the "people" excludes without consideration all immigrants, Spanish or Portuguese, Algerian or Moroccan, Malian or Senegalese, whom we know occupy a more important place in the population of industrial workers than the imaginary proletariat.[3]

It would be sufficient to submit to similar examination the populations that supposedly produce or consume so-called popular culture to find the same confusion in the partial coherence that the *implicit definitions* almost always conceal: the "lowlife," which plays a central role in the case of "popular language," would be excluded here, as well as the lumpenproletariat, while the elimination of rural workers would no longer be a given, even though the coexistence of the inevitable urban working class and the rural populations is not without difficulties. In the case of "popular art," as an examination of this other objectification of "popular" would clearly show, the "people," those "muses of the popular arts and traditions" at least until recent times, are reduced to peasants and rural artisans. And what does "popular medicine" or "popular religion" mean? In these cases, we can no more do without the rural populations, men or women, than we can do without the "toughs" in the case of "popular language."

In their efforts to treat it as a "language"—that is to say with all the rigor ordinarily reserved for the legitimate language—all those who have tried to describe or to write in the *pop.*, linguists and writers alike, have condemned themselves to producing artifacts bearing almost no relationship to the ordinary speech that the speakers most estranged from the legitimate language use in their internal exchanges.[4] So it is that, in order to conform to the dominant dictionary model whereby only words attested "with appreciable frequency and over long durations" are included, the authors of nonconventional French dictionaries rely exclusively on texts.[5] And thus by making a selection within a selection, they subject the speech in question to an essential alteration with regard to the frequencies that make all the difference between the kinds of speech and the more or less strained markets.[6] They forget, among other things, that to write speech, like that of the working classes, that is without *literary* intention (and not to transcribe it or record it), it is necessary to be outside of situations and even of the social condition in which it is spoken, and that interest in the "coinages," or even the very fact of selective recollection, excluding all that is encountered in the standard language *as well*, overturns the structure of frequencies.

If, despite their incoherences and their uncertainties, and also thanks to them, the notions belonging to the family of the "popular" can prove so useful, and even in scholarly discourse, it is because they are deeply entrenched in the network of confused representations that social subjects engender, for the needs of ordinary knowledge of the social world, and for which the logic is that of mythical reason. The vision of the social world, and above all the *perception of others*, of their corporal *hexis*, the form and volume of their bodies, and especially of their faces, and also their voices, their pronunciation and vocabulary, is organized in effect according to interconnected and partially independent oppositions, about which one can get an idea by making an inventory of the expressive resources collected and preserved in the language, especially in the *system of adjective pairs* that users of the legitimate language employ to classify others and to judge their *quality*, and in which the term designating the properties attributed to the dominants always represents positive value.[7]

If the social sciences must make a privileged place for the science of ordinary knowledge of the social world, it is not only in critical intention and in view of ridding the thinking about the social world of all the presuppositions that it tends to accept through ordinary words and the objects that they construct ("popular language," "slang," "patois," and so on). It is also that this practical knowledge, against which the science must be constructed—and first of all by endeavoring to objectify it—forms an integral part of the very world that the science aims to know: it contributes to the making of that world by contributing to the vision that agents can have of it and by thus orienting their actions, in particular those that aim at conserving or transforming it. That is why a rigorous science of the spontaneous sociolinguistics that agents put to work to anticipate the reactions of others and to impose the representation that they want to give of themselves would permit, among other things, an understanding of a good part of what, in linguistic practice, is the object or the product of conscious intervention, individual or collective, spontaneous or institutionalized: as for example all the *corrections* that speakers impose on themselves or that are imposed on them—at home or at school—on the basis of practical knowledge, partially registered in the language itself (*accent pointu*—"northern accent," *marseillais*—"Marseilles accent," *faubourien*—"Paris working-class accent," and so on), of the correspondences between linguistic differences and social differences and beginning with a more or less conscious pinpointing of linguistic traits marked or remarked upon as imperfect or incorrect (notably by the form, "Say . . . , don't say . . ." in all linguistic customaries) or, alternatively, as distinguishing and refined.[8]

The notion of "popular language" is one of the products of the application of the dualist taxonomies that structure the social world according to categories of high and low ("low" language), delicate or coarse (coarse words) or crude (crude jokes), distinguished or vulgar, rare or common, formal or casual, in short, categories of culture and nature (don't we speak of slang as *langue verte*—literally "green language" and "raw words"?). These are the mythical categories that introduce a distinct cleavage in the continuum of kinds of speech, ignoring, for example, all the overlapping between the casual speech of the dominant speakers (*fam.*) and the strained speech of the dominated speakers (that observers like Bauche or Frei list as *pop.*) and especially the extreme diversity in the kinds of speech that are universally consigned to the negative category of "popular language."[9]

But through a sort of paradoxical reduplication, which is one of the standard effects of symbolic domination, the dominated themselves, or at least certain fractions of them, can apply to their own social universe principles of division (such as strong vs. weak or submissive; intelligent vs. sensitive or sensual; hard vs. soft or flexible; straight or direct vs. crooked, sly, or false; and so on) that reproduce in their order the fundamental structure of the system of dominant oppositions in matters of language.[10] This representation of the social world adopts the essence of the dominant vision through the opposition between virility and docility, strength and weakness, real men (the *durs*, the *mecs*) and the other feminine or effeminate beings doomed to submission and contempt.[11] Slang, which has been made into the "popular language" par excellence, is the product of this reduplication that brings to bear on "popular language" itself the principles of division of which it is a product. There is a vague feeling that linguistic conformity conceals a form of acknowledgment and submission, enough to call into doubt the virility of those men who conform.[12] Added to that is the active pursuit of a distinctive deviation that constitutes style. And together these lead to refusing to "overdo it," which leads to rejecting the most strongly marked aspects of the dominant speech, and notably the pronunciations and the most strained syntactical forms, as well as simultaneously pursuing expressiveness, based on the transgression of dominant censures—notably in matters of sexuality—and with the intention of distinguishing oneself from the ordinary forms of expression.[13] The transgression of official norms, linguistic or otherwise, is directed at least as much against the "ordinary" dominated who submit to them as it is against the dominant or, a fortiori, against the domination as such. Linguistic license is part of the *work of representation* and of presenting what the "toughs," especially adolescents, must provide to impose on others and themselves the image of the *mec* who has seen it all and is ready for anything and who refuses to give in to feelings or submit to the weaknesses of feminine sensitivity. And in fact, even if it can, in divulging itself, encounter the proclivity of all the dominated to return the distinction, that is to say the specific difference, to the common genre, that is to say to the universality of the biological, through irony, sarcasm, or parody, the systematic degradation of emotional, moral, or aesthetic values, where all the analysts have recognized the deep "intention" of the slang lexicon, is first of all an affirmation of aristocratism.

As a distinguished form—even in the eyes of some of the dominants—of "vulgar" language, slang is the product of a search for distinction but dominated and condemned by this fact to produce paradoxical effects, which we cannot understand when we want to contain them within the alternative of resistance or submission that controls ordinary thinking on "popular language" (or "popular culture"). Indeed it is enough to exit the logic of the mythical vision to perceive the counterproductive effects that are inherent to any dominated position: when the pursuit of the dominated for distinction leads them to affirm what distinguishes them, that is to say, whatever it is in the name of which they are dominated and constituted as vulgar, according to a logic analogical to the one that leads stigmatized groups to claim the stigmata as fundamental to their identity, is it necessary to speak of resistance? And when, alternatively, they work to lose what marks them as vulgar, and to appropriate what would allow them to be assimilated, is it necessary to speak of submission?

* * *

In order to escape the effects of the dualistic mode of thought that leads to opposing a "standard" language, the measure of all language, to a "popular" language, it is necessary to return to the model of all linguistic production and rediscover there the principle of the extreme diversity in kinds of speech that results in the diversity of possible combinations among the various classes of linguistic habitus and markets. Among the determining factors of the habitus that seem relevant from the perspective, on the one hand, of the propensity to recognize (in both senses) the constituent *censures* of the dominant markets or to profit from the *obligatory freedoms* that certain free markets offer and, on the other hand, of the capacity to satisfy the requirements of one or the other, we can thus retain: the *sex*, a principle of very different relationships in various possible markets—and in the dominant market in particular; the *generation*, that is to say the familial and especially scholastic mode of generation of linguistic competence; the *social position*, characterized notably from the perspective of the social composition of the work environment and the socially homogeneous (with the dominated) or heterogeneous (with the dominant—in the case, for example, of service staff) exchanges that they foster; the social *origin*, *rural* or *urban* and, in this case, old or recent; and finally the *ethnic* origin.

It is obviously among men and, within that group, among the youngest and—at present and especially potentially—the least integrated into the economic and social order, like the adolescents coming from immigrant families, that we encounter the most marked refusal of the submission and docility that adopting legitimate ways of speaking implies. The moral code of force that finds its fulfillment in the cult of violence and semi-suicidal games, motorcycles, alcohol, or hard drugs, where the relationship to the future for those who have nothing to look forward to in the future is affirmed, is no doubt only one of the ways of making a virtue of necessity. The flaunted stance of realism and cynicism, the rejection of feeling and sensitivity, identified with feminine or effeminate sentimentality, the kind of duty to be tough, for oneself as for others, that leads to the desperate effronteries of the aristocratism of the pariah, are a way of taking one's part in a dead-end world dominated by poverty and the law of the jungle, discrimination, and violence, where morality and sensitivity are entirely without profit.[14] The moral code that constitutes transgression imposes the duty of displaying one's resistance to the official norms, linguistic or otherwise, which can only be continually sustained at the cost of extraordinary tension and, especially for adolescents, with the constant reinforcement of the group. Like popular realism, which assumes and produces the adjustment of hopes to chances, it constitutes a mechanism of defense and survival: those compelled to position themselves outside the law to obtain satisfactions that others obtain within the limits of legality know only too well the cost of revolt. As Paul E. Willis has clearly seen, the poses and postures of bravado (toward authority, for example, and above all toward the police) can coexist with a deep conformism to all that concerns hierarchies, and not only between the sexes, and ostentatious toughness that human respect imposes does not in the least exclude nostalgia for solidarity, indeed even for affection, which, simultaneously fulfilled and repressed by the highly censored exchanges of the gang, is expressed or revealed in moments of

abandon.[15] Slang—and this, along with the effect of symbolic imposition, is one of the reasons for its diffusion well beyond the limits
of the "lowlife" strictly speaking—constitutes *one* of the exemplary,
and if we may say so, ideal, expressions—which political expression proper must be able to reckon with, indeed even employ—of
the vision, essentially constructed against feminine (or effeminate)
"weakness" or "submission," that the men most lacking in economic
and cultural capital hold of their masculine identity and of a social
world entirely situated under the sign of toughness.[16]

All the same we must be careful not to ignore the profound transformations in function and meaning undergone by borrowed words
or phrases when they pass into the ordinary speech of everyday
exchanges. That is why some of the most typical products of the aristocratic cynicism of the "toughs" can, in their common use, function as kinds of neutralized and neutralizing conventions that allow
men to express, within the limits of a very strict propriety, affection,
love, and friendship, or simply just to name beloved beings, parents,
son, or wife (the more or less ironic use of reference terms like "the
old lady," "queen mother," or "the missus" allowing men to avoid, for
example, expressions like "my wife" or the simple first name, felt to
be too familiar).[17]

At the opposite extreme in the hierarchy of dispositions toward
the legitimate language, we would no doubt find the youngest and
most schooled among the women who, however tied by occupation
or by marriage to the universe of agents weakly endowed with economic or cultural capital, are clearly sensitive to the demands of the
dominant market and are able to respond to it, which makes them
similar to the petite bourgeoisie. As for the effect of generation, it
essentially merges with the effect of changes in the mode of generation, that is to say, access to the school system, which clearly represents the most important differentiation factor between the ages.

All the same, it is not certain that the action of schooling exercises the effect of homogenization of linguistic abilities that it

assigns itself and that one would be tempted to attribute to it. First, because the scholastic norms of expression, when they are accepted, can remain circumscribed in their application to school products, oral and especially written; second, because school tends to distribute students in classes as homogeneous as possible with regard to scholastic criteria, and as a correlative, from the perspective of social criteria, in such a way that the peer group tends to exercise effects that, as one descends in the social hierarchy of educational establishments and sections and thus in social origins, are more and more strongly opposed to those that pedagogical action can produce; and finally, because paradoxically, by creating long-lasting, homogeneous groups of adolescents at odds with the school system and, through it, with the social order, and placed in a situation of semi-inactivity and prolonged irresponsibility,[18] the sections to which the children of the most destitute classes are relegated—notably the sons of immigrants, especially North Africans—have undoubtedly contributed to providing the most favorable conditions for the development of a kind of "delinquent culture" that, among other ways, is expressed in speech at odds with the norms of legitimate language.

No one can completely ignore linguistic or cultural law, and every time they enter into an exchange with those who possess legitimate competence, and especially when they find themselves in official situations, the dominated are condemned to a practical, corporal recognition of the laws of price formation most unfavorable to their linguistic productions, which condemns them to a more or less desperate effort toward correction or toward *silence*. It remains true that the markets they confront can be classified according to their degree of autonomy, from the most completely subject to the dominant norms (like those that are imposed in relationships with the legal, medical, or school systems) to the most completely free of those laws (like those that are constituted in prisons or youth gangs). The affirmation of a linguistic counter-legitimacy and, at the same time, the production of discourse founded on the more or less deliberate ignorance of conventions and proprieties characteristic of the dominant markets are only possible within the limits of the *free markets*, regulated by the laws of price formation that are exclusive to them, that is to say, in the spaces belonging to the dominated classes, haunts or refuges of the excluded from which the dominant are in fact excluded, at least symbolically, and for the appointed possessors of the social and linguistic competence that is recognized in those markets. The slang of the "lowlife," as actual transgression of the fundamental principles of cultural legitimacy, constitutes an affirmation consistent with a social and cultural identity not only different but opposed, and the vision of the world expressed by it represents the *limit* toward which the (masculine) members of the dominated classes tend in linguistic exchanges *internal to the class*, and most especially in the most controlled and sustained of those exchanges, as those in bars and cafés, which are completely dominated by the values of force and masculinity, one of the only principles of effective resistance, along with politics, against the dominant ways of speaking and acting.

The internal markets distinguish themselves according to the *tension* that characterizes them and, at the same time, according to the degree of censorship that they impose, and one can hypothesize that the *frequency* of the most affected forms (of slang) declines as the tension of the markets and the linguistic competence of the speakers decline. It is minimal in *private* and familiar exchanges (exchanges within the family ranking first among these) where independence in relationship to the norms of legitimate speech is marked especially by the more or less complete freedom to *ignore* the conventions and proprieties of the dominant speech, and it undoubtedly reaches its maximum in *public* exchanges (almost exclusively masculine) that impose a veritable *stylistic affectation*, as in the verbal jousts and ostentatious outbidding of some café conversations.

***

Despite the enormous simplification that it assumes, this model makes apparent the extreme diversity of the discourses that are practically engendered in the relationship between the various linguistic competences corresponding to the various combinations of characteristics attached to the producers and the various classes of markets. But more importantly, it allows us to draw up the *program of methodical observation* and to constitute as such the most significant scenarios in which are situated all the linguistic productions of the speakers most lacking in linguistic capital. That is, first of all, the forms of discourse presented by the virtuosos in the most strained—that is to say public—of the free markets and, in particular, slang; secondly, the expressions produced for the dominant markets, that is to say the private exchanges between dominated and dominant, or for *official* situations, and that can take the form of embarrassed or broken speech through the effect of intimidation or of *silence*, the only form of expression that is left, very often, to the dominated; and last of all, the discourses produced for familiar and private exchanges—for example between women—these last two categories of discourse always being excluded by those who, characterizing linguistic productions by the characteristics of the speakers alone, must according to good logic put them into the category of "popular language."

The effect of censorship that any relatively strained market exercises is seen in the fact that the words exchanged in public places reserved in fact (at least during certain hours) to adult men of the working classes, like some bars or cafés, are heavily ritualized and subject to strict rules: one does not go to the bar just to drink but also to participate actively in a collective diversion capable of providing the participants with a feeling of freedom in relationship to the daily necessities, and of producing an atmosphere of social euphoria and economic license to which the consumption of alcohol can clearly only contribute. One is there to laugh and to make others laugh, and each participant must, according to his means, throw into the exchange his jokes and witticisms, or at the very least make his contribution to the festivities by reinforcing others' successes with his laughter and his approving exclamations (*Ah! celui-là!*— "Yes! That's it!"). Possessing a talent for always being good for a laugh, being able to embody, at the cost of the conscious and constant work of pursuit and accumulation, the ideal of the "life of the party" who brings to his accomplishment an approved form of sociability, is a very precious form of capital. That is what the good bar owner finds in the mastery of expressive conventions suitable to this market, jokes, good stories, wordplay, that his permanent and central position allows him to acquire and display, and also in his special knowledge of the rules of the game and distinctive characteristics of each player, first names, last names, odd habits, shortcomings, specialties, and talents that he can turn to good account, the resources necessary for prompting, maintaining, and also containing, through incitements, boasts, or discrete calls to order, the exchanges capable of producing the atmosphere of social effervescence that his clients are seeking and that they themselves must supply.[19] The quality of the conversation provided depends upon the quality of the participants, which itself depends upon the quality of the conversation, and so upon the one who is at the center of it and who must know how to deny the mercenary relationship by affirming his will and his ability to join the circuit of exchanges as an ordinary participant— with a "free round" or a "drink on the house" offered to regulars— and thus to contribute to the suspension of economic necessities and social constraints that is expected from the collective worship of the good life.[20]

We understand that the discourse that circulates on this market only gives the appearance of total freedom and absolute naturalness to those who are unaware of its rules or principles. That is why its eloquence, which an outside perspective apprehends as a kind of unbridled verve, is neither more nor less free within its genre than the improvisations of academic eloquence. Neither is it unaware of trying for effect, or of the audience's attention and reactions, or of rhetorical strategies aimed at winning the audience's favor or indulgence. It relies on proven but appropriate schemas of invention and expression to give those who do not possess them the feeling of witnessing dazzling displays of analytical acuity or political or psychological lucidity. Through the tremendous redundancy tolerated by its rhetoric, through the place it gives to the repetition of ritual forms and formulas that are the required demonstrations of a "good education," through its systematic recourse to concrete images from the familiar world, through the obsessional obstinacy that it takes to reaffirm, even in their formal renewal, the fundamental values of the group, this discourse expresses and reinforces a profoundly stable and rigid vision of the world. In this system of obvious facts, tirelessly reaffirmed and collectively guaranteed, that assigns to each class of agents its essence, and thus its place and rank, the representation of the division of labor between the sexes occupies a central place, perhaps because the cult of masculinity, that is to say of toughness, physical force, and gruff coarseness, established by elective rejection of effeminate refinement, is one of the most effective ways of struggling against the cultural inferiority in which all those who feel deprived of cultural capital find themselves, whether they are otherwise rich in economic capital, like the merchants, or not.[21]

At the opposite extreme in the class of free markets, the market of exchanges among familiars, and especially among women, distinguishes itself in that the very idea of affectation and effect is almost absent there, so that the discourse circulating in it differs in form, as we have seen, from that of the public exchanges in bars and cafés; it is in the logic of deprivation, more than of rejection, that it defines itself in relation to legitimate discourse. As for the dominant markets, public and official or private, to the most economically and culturally deprived, they pose problems so difficult that if we confined ourselves to the definition of speech based on the social characteristics of the speakers, the definition implicitly adopted by the tenants of "popular language," we would have to say that the most frequent form of this language is silence. In fact, it is again according to the logic of the division of labor between the sexes that the contradiction resulting from the necessity to confront the dominant markets without conforming to the affectation of correction is resolved. Because it is acknowledged (and first of all by women, who can pretend to deplore it) that a man is defined by the right and duty of constancy to himself that is a component of his identity ("he is the way he is") and that he can confine himself to a silence that allows him to safeguard his masculine pride, it often becomes incumbent upon the woman, socially defined as flexible and submissive by nature, to make the necessary effort to confront perilous situations, to meet with the doctor, to describe symptoms and discuss treatments, to approach the school teacher or Social Security, and so on.[22] It follows that the "mistakes" that are based on an unfortunate affectation of correction or a misdirected concern for distinction and that, like all distorted words, especially medical ones, are mercilessly picked out by the petite bourgeoisie—and by "popular language" grammars— are undoubtedly very often owed to women (for which they can be mocked by "their" men—which is again a way of relegating women to their "nature" as fusspots).[23]

In fact, even in this case, demonstrations of docility are never without ambivalence, and they always threaten to revert into aggressiveness at the least rebuff, at the least sign of irony or distance, which converts them into the tributes required by statutory dependence. One who, upon entering into too unequal a social relationship, too visibly adopts the appropriated language and manners exposes oneself to being forced to conceive of and experience elective reverence as obligatory submission and self-interested servility. The image of the domestic, which owes its conspicuous conformity to the dominant norms of verbal etiquette and service uniforms, haunts all relationships between the dominated and dominant, and notably the service exchanges, as made evident by the almost insoluble problems

that "remuneration" poses. That is why ambivalence toward dominants and their lifestyle, so common among men performing service
functions, which wavers between the inclination to nervous conformity and the temptation to allow themselves familiarities and to
degrade the dominants by raising themselves to their level, undoubtedly represents the truth and the limit of the relationship that the
men most lacking in linguistic capital and vowed to the alternative
of coarseness and servility maintain with the dominant mode of
expression.[24] Paradoxically, it is only when the solemnity of the occasion justifies, in their eyes, situating themselves within a more noble
register, without feeling ridiculous or servile, that they can adopt the
language that is more conventional but the only one suited to their
meaning, to saying serious things; for example, to express their love
or display their sympathy in mourning. That is to say, in the very
cases when the dominant norms require that one abandon ready-
made conventions and formulas for demonstrating the strength and
sincerity of one's feelings.

* * *

Thus it appears that the linguistic and cultural productions of the dominated vary profoundly according to their inclination and aptitude for
taking advantage of the regulated freedoms that the free market offers or
for accepting the restraints that the dominant markets impose. Which
explains how, in the polymorphous reality obtained by considering all
the kinds of speech produced by all the markets through all the categories of producers, all those who feel they have the right or duty to speak
of the "people" can find an objective medium for their interests or their
fantasies.

3

"WE, THE PEOPLE"

THOUGHTS ON FREEDOM OF ASSEMBLY

JUDITH BUTLER

There are many examples of people coming together, forming a way of speaking as a collective, and demanding a change in policy or a dissolution of a government. Tahrir Square has become emblematic of this assembly of bodies on the street who first demanded the dissolution of the Mubarak regime and then continued, in different configurations, to arrive on the street en masse to object to various policies of the transitional regime, to the appointment of officials known to have engaged in torture in the previous regime, opposing the accelerated pace by which a new constitution was forged and objecting most recently to the dissolution of the court system by the president's unilateral decree. What kind of "we" is this who assembles in the street and asserts itself sometimes by speech or action, by gesture, but more often than not by coming together as a group of bodies in public space, visible, audible, tangible, exposed, persistent, and interdependent. Although we often think that the speech act by which "we, the people" consolidates its popular sovereignty is one that issues from such an assembly, it is perhaps more appropriate to say that the assembly is already speaking and is already an enactment of popular sovereignty. The "we" voiced in language is already enacted by the assembly of bodies, their gestures and movements, their vocalizations, and their ways of acting in concert, to cite Hannah Arendt.[1]

The right to exercise the freedom of assembly, sometimes understood as the freedom of association, is by now well documented in international law.[2] The International Labour Organization makes explicit that the right of assembly (or association) is tied to the rights of collective bargaining.[3] In some human rights discourses, the freedom of assembly is described as a fundamental form of freedom that deserves protection by any government without interference (the use of police and judicial powers to enact indefinite detention or arrest, harassment, assault, or disappearances). Freedom of assembly does not depend upon that protection in those cases when the protective power of the state is contested by such an assembly or when a specific state has contravened the right of assembly such that its population can no longer freely congregate without threat of state interference. So the freedom of assembly is something other than a specific right protected by existing national or international law, including human rights law. Indeed, the freedom of assembly may well be a precondition of politics itself.

How, then, do we think about the freedom of assembly and popular sovereignty? Although elected officials are supposed to represent popular sovereignty (or the "popular will" more specifically) by virtue of having been elected by a majority of the population, it does not follow that popular sovereignty is in any way exhausted by the electoral process or that elections fully transfer sovereignty from the populace to its elected representatives. The populace remains separate from those elected and can continue to contest the conditions and results of elections, as well as the actions of elected officials. So "popular sovereignty" certainly translates into elected power on the occasion of a vote, but that is never a full translation. Something remains untranslatable about popular sovereignty since it can surely bring down regimes as well as elect them. As much as popular sovereignty legitimates parliamentary forms of power, it also retains the power to delegitimate those same forms. If parliamentary forms of power require popular sovereignty, they also surely fear it, for there is something about popular sovereignty that runs counter to, and exceeds, every parliamentary form that it institutes. Even an elected regime can be brought to a halt or overcome by that assembly of people who speak "in the name of the people," enacting the very "we" that holds final legitimating power under conditions of democratic rule. In other words, the conditions of democratic rule depend finally upon an exercise of popular sovereignty that is never fully contained by any particular democratic order. Popular sovereignty might be understood as an extra-parliamentary power without which no parliament can function, and which threatens every parliament with dysfunction or even dissolution. We can call it an "anarchist" energy or a permanent principle of revolution within democratic orders. In either case, it depends upon a set of bodies assembled and assembling, whose actions effectively constitute themselves as "the people."

Of course, it is never really the case that all of the possible people who are represented by "the people" show up to claim that they are the people! So "we, the people" always has its constitutive outside, as we know. It is thus surely not the fact that the "we" fairly and fully represents all the people; it cannot, even though it can strive for more inclusive aims. Indeed, those who assemble as the "we" who are "the people" are not representing the people but providing the legitimating ground for those who do come to represent the people through elections. The people who are the "we" do something other than represent themselves; they constitute themselves as the people, and this act of self-making or self-constitution is not the same as any form of representation. Something nonrepresentative and nearly tautological thus becomes the basis of democratic forms of government—popular sovereignty is thus a way of forming a people through an act of self-designation. This act of self-designating and self-constituting forms an assembly that articulates itself as the "people." Popular sovereignty is thus a form of reflexive self-making that is separate from the very representative regime it legitimates. It cannot do this work of legitimation unless it is independent of any particular regime.

In what sense is popular sovereignty a performative exercise?

It would seem, then, that "we, the people" is first and foremost a speech act that is self-designating and self-constituting. Someone says "we" along with someone else, or some group says it together, and when they say it, they seek to constitute themselves as "the people" at that moment. So, considered as a speech act, "we, the people" is an enunciation that seeks to bring about the social plurality it names. It does not describe that plurality but seeks to bring about the social plurality that speaks it. It would seem, then, that a linguistic form of autogenesis is at work in the expression "we, the people"; it seems to be a rather magical act, or at least one that compels us to believe in the magical nature of the performative.[4] Of course, "we, the people" starts a longer declaration of wants and desires, or intended acts, and political claims. It is a preamble, so it prepares the way for a specific set of assertions. It is a phrase that gets us ready for a substantive political claim, and yet, in this volume, we are asked to pause at this way of starting up the sentence and ask whether a political claim is already being made, or is in the making. It is perhaps impossible for all the people who might say "we, the people" at the same time to speak that phrase in unison. And if somehow an assembled group were to yell out "we, the people," as sometimes happens in the assemblies of the Occupy movement, it is a brief and transitory moment, one in which a single person speaks at the same time that others speak, and some unintended plural sounding results from that concerted plural action, that speech act spoken in common.

But let us admit that such a moment of literally speaking in unison, and naming ourselves as "the people," rarely happens quite like that—simultaneous and plural. After all, the declaration of "we, the people" in the United States is a citation, and the phrase is never fully freed of its citationality. The Constitution begins with such a phrase, one that authorizes the writers to speak for the people more generally. It is a phrase that establishes political authority at the same time that it declares a form of popular sovereignty bound by no one political authority. Popular sovereignty can give itself (in assent) and withdraw itself (in dissent or in revolution), which means that every regime is dependent upon popular sovereignty being given if it hopes to base its legitimacy on something other than coercion.

The speech act, however punctual, is nevertheless inserted in a citational chain, and that means that the temporal conditions for making the speech act precede and exceed the momentary occasion of its enunciation. And for yet another reason, the speech act, however illocutionary, is not fully tethered to the moment of its enunciation: the plurality designated and produced by the utterance cannot all assemble in the same place to speak at the same time, so it is both a spatially and temporally extended phenomenon. When and where popular sovereignty—the self-legislative power of the people—is "declared," or rather "declares itself," it is not exactly at an instant but instead through a series of speech acts or performative enactments. We can postulate the scene of a public assembly in which everyone speaks in one voice, but this scene is both abstract and somewhat frightening—invoking a kind of *Gleichschaltung* that suggests a fascist march or militaristic chant of some kind. "We, the people" does not presuppose or make a unity but founds or institutes a set of debates about who the people are and what they want.

I take it that we do not really want every person speaking in the exact same way when popular sovereignty is being asserted, or even "saying" the same words. (Which language would be used for such an idea of concerted plural expression? And what form of hegemony would that install?) And yet, "we, the people" is a phrase that we take to be emblematic of a form of popular sovereignty that assumes that the people can and do act together to name themselves and so to collect themselves in a plural political form. This does not mean that they agree with one another but only that they understand that the process of self-making is a collective or shared one. When someone tries to mobilize "we, the people," we look over to see who says it, whether they have a right to say it, but whether, in saying it, their speech act will be effective, gathering forth the people in the very saying. The phrase does not tell us who the people are, but it marks the form of self-constitution in which that debate over who they are and should be begins to take place.

So if we were following J. L. Austin, "we, the people" would be considered an illocutionary speech act that constitutes its object (itself) at the moment of its enunciation.[5] And yet, as citational, I would suggest that is actually constituted time and again, and always only partially, through a sequence or a cluster of performative enactments that turn out not always to be a simultaneous and plural form of self-designation. As we perhaps can see, "we, the people" is a phrase, then, that conducts an implicit critique of the magical powers of the enunciatory act, the illocutionary performative. It is rarely spoken as such, and yet it speaks through other acts. And if we imagine that a group must first assemble in a particular place, a public square or some equivalent, in order to proclaim "we, the people," then *we fail to recognize that the act of assembling and reassembling is already doing the work of the phrase*; in other words, assembling is already a performative political enactment even if it is prior to, and apart from, any particular speech act. Implied by such a notion is that bodies assembled together to assert their plural existence are already engaged in self-designation and the exercise of popular sovereignty, lending or withdrawing their support, declaring their independence from the regimes that depend upon it for legitimacy. The performative is thus outside of electoral power at the same time that it functions as its legitimation. Enacted by bodies arriving in a space and time together, or through circuitries that connect diverse spaces and times, political performatives do not have to be spoken in unison, or even in the same language, to be constituting themselves as "a people." And when they assemble, or scatter and then reassemble, the performative is no longer a punctual "act" or discrete occasion of enunciation (although it can sometimes surely take that form). So, then, we are left with this question: *does the speech act by which "we, the people" is declared finally not take place in speech, and prove to be something other than a single act?*

I propose to think about the assembly of bodies as a performative enactment and so to suggest not only that (a) popular sovereignty is a performative exercise, but (b) it necessarily involves a performative enactment of bodies. First, I propose that we have to understand the idea of popular sovereignty that "we, the people" seeks to secure. In the Declaration of Independence, as Derrida has shown, there is already a kind of stumbling that takes place.[6] If the "we" who hold these truths to be self-evident are the people, then we are already in a bit of a bind. A performative declaration seeks to bring about those truths, but if they are "self-evident" then they are precisely the kinds of truths that do not need to be brought about at all. Either they are performatively induced or they are self-evident, but to bring about that which is self-evident seems paradoxical. We could say that a set of truths is being brought into being, or we could say that we found those truths somewhere and that we did not bring them into being. Or we can say that the kind of truths at issue here have to be declared as self-evident for that self-evidence to be known. In other words, they have to be made evident, which means that they are not self-evident. This circularity seems to risk contradiction or tautology, but perhaps the truths only become evident in the manner in which they are declared. In other words, the performative enactment of the truth is the way of making evident that very truth, since the truth in question is not pre-given or static but enacted or exercised through a particular kind of plural action. If it is the very capacity for plural action that is at stake in claiming popular sovereignty, then there is no way to "show" this truth outside of the plural and invariably conflictual enactment we call self-constitution.

If the plural subject is constituted in the course of its performative action, then it is not already constituted, which means that whatever form it has prior to its performative exercise is not the same as the form it takes as it acts, and after it has acted. The "we" effects a certain gathering. At the same time, it is only when bodies gather in some particular configuration of space and time that the "we" comes into being, even if it is not explicitly spoken. So how do we then understand this movement of gathering, which is durational and implies occasional, periodic, or definitive forms of scattering? It is not one act, but a convergence of actions different from one another, a form of political sociality irreducible to conformity. Even when a crowd speaks together, they have to gather in close enough proximity to hear another's voice, to pace one's own vocalization, to achieve rhythm and harmony to a sufficient degree, and so to establish a relation both auditory and corporeal with those with whom some signifying action or speech act is undertaken. We start to speak *now* and stop *now*. We start to move *now*, or more or less at a given time, but certainly not as a single organism. We try to stop all at once, but some keep moving, and others move and rest at their own pace. Temporal seriality and coordination, bodily proximity, auditory range, coordinated vocalization—all of these constitute essential dimensions of assembly and demonstration. And they are all presupposed by the speech act that enunciates "we, the people"; they are the complex elements of the *occasion* of its enunciation.

The body has always been part of that occasion. Let us recall that the illocutionary act is characterized as one that brings about effects on the occasion of its enunciation. This does not mean that enunciation is its own occasion, since any enunciation presupposes a specific convergence of spatial, temporal, and sensible fields. Indeed, the occasion in which "we, the people" is enunciated presupposes an embodied and plural political sociality. Even when we thought, if we ever did, that the speech act was *purely* linguistic, it depended upon a model of vocalization that required the throat and mouth, breathing, a bodily organism comported in a given way, a circumscribed auditory field, a zone of proximity such that bodies close enough to hear or see or sense in some other way what each was doing and saying in order to try to do and say something together; speech is itself a movement, and "movement" carried two basic senses: bodily mobility and political organization.

Is there, then, any speech act that brings forth "we, the people" that is not a bodily and political movement of some kind? Does that speech act always presuppose, gather, and enact a body politic? On the one hand, if we take vocalization as the model of the speech act, then the body is surely presupposed as the organ of speech, both the organic condition and vehicle of speech. The body is not transmuted into pure thought as it speaks, but signifies the organic conditions for verbalization. So if speech is conceptualized restrictively as a vocalized speech act, there is no speech without the organ of speech, which means that there is surely no speech act without the organic. But what does the organic dimension of speech do to the claims made in speech, and on behalf of speech? If one assumes that speech reflects consciousness and, in particular, the "intention" of the speaker, then intention is figured as a cognitive moment represented by speech; in turn, speech is understood as corresponding to this prior cognitive content. Shoshana Felman has made this clear in the *Le scandale du corps parlant* that precisely because speech is impossible without the organic, even the speech act that seeks to convey a purely cognitive intention cannot circumvent the organic body.[7] The most purely ideal intention manifest in speech is impossible without its organic condition.

So just as there is no purely linguistic speech act separated from bodily acts, there is no purely conceptual moment of thought that does away with its own organic condition. And this tells us something about what it means to say "we, the people" since whether it is written in a text or uttered on the street, it designates an assembly in the act of designating and forming itself. It acts on itself as it acts, and a corporeal condition of plurality is indexed whether or not it appears on the occasion of the utterance. That bodily condition, plural and dynamic, is a constitutive dimension of that occasion.

And we can add the following: the "organic" is no more pure than the conceptual intention it seeks to convey, since it is always organized in some way, belonging not to this or that discrete substance but to a cluster of relations, gestures, and movements that constitute its social sense. So, then, what other kinds of bodily actions and inactions, gestures, movements, and modes of coordination and organization can condition and constitute the speech act, no longer understood restrictively as vocalization? Sounds are but one way to signify in common—singing, chanting, declaring, beating drums or pots, or pounding against a prison or separation wall. How do all these kinds of acts "speak" in ways that index another sense of the organic and the political, one that might be understood as the performative enactment of assembly itself?

* * *

The performative enactment of "we, the people" happens prior to any vocalization of that particular phrase. The phrase is embodied before it is spoken, and even when it is spoken, it remains embodied. The phrase cannot be thought apart from its embodiment. And though "we, the people" is that act, or series of acts, by which an assembly of some kind designates and forms itself in space and time, it is also prior to any specific demand for justice or equality. So demands emerge only after an assembly designates itself as a people, and that self-formation is prior to any particular claim made in the name of the people. "We, the people" is a performative enactment without demands, though it surely gives rise to demands that depend fundamentally upon that embodied and performative institution of the people in its plurality.[8]

The embodied character of the people proves quite important to the kinds of demands that are made. When, for instance, wealth is accumulated among 2 percent of the population and increasing numbers of people lose their homes and employment, then the people are clearly divided along class lines and economic power is distributed in radically unequal ways. When those who face accelerating prospects of precarity take to the streets and begin their claim with "we, the people," then they are asserting that they, those who appear and speak there, are identified as "the people." They are working against oblivion. The phrase does not imply that those who profit are not "the people," and it does not necessarily imply a simple sense of inclusion: "we are the people, too." Rather, it asserts a form of equality in the face of increasing inequality, and it does this not simply by uttering that phrase but by embodying equality to whatever extent that proves possible, constituting an assembly of the people on the grounds of equality. One might say they are asserting inequality in the midst of inequality, and this is vain and useless, since their act is only symbolic, and true economic equality continues to become more elusive for those whose debts are astronomical and employment prospects foreclosed. And yet it seems that the embodiment of equality in the practices of assembly, the insistence on interdependency, the commonly held ground, all start to put into the world a version of equality that is rapidly vanishing in other quarters. The point is not to regard the body merely as an instrument for making a political claim but to let this body, the plurality of bodies, become the precondition of all further political claims.

Indeed, in the politics of the street that has been with us in the last years, in the Occupy movement, Tahrir Square, Puerta del Sol, the basic requirements of the body are at the center of political mobilizations—*those requirements are, in fact, publicly enacted prior to any set of political demands.* And we could certainly make a list of those demands: bodies require food and shelter, protection from injury and violence, the freedom to move, to work, to have access to health care; bodies require other bodies for support and for survival. It matters, of course, what age those bodies are, and whether they are able-bodied, since in all forms of dependency, bodies require not just one other person but social systems of support that are complexly human and technical.

In a world in which the bodily life of increasing numbers of people is proving to be highly precarious, bodies emerge together on the pavement or the dirt or along the wall that separates them from their land—this assembly, which can include virtual participants, still assumes a set of interlocking locations for a plural set of bodies. And in this way, the bodies belong to the pavement, the ground, the architecture, and the technology by which they live. Thus we cannot speak about bodies without the environments, the machines, and the complex systems of social interdependency that are their conditions of support; no body survives, much less flourishes, without conditions of support. This fact, the condition of life, is enacted, shown; it emerges from the oblivion to which it is increasingly relegated. And though it seems to imply several political claims, the making of the plural body in plain view, and in defiance of those forms of police and economic power that would sequester it again, lays down the basic conditions for further political claims. If we were to come to enumerate all the requirements of the body, would we struggle only for those requirements to be met? Or do we struggle as well for bodies to thrive and for lives to become livable?

Perhaps it is possible to distinguish between a condition of politics and its various demands. Arendt famously remarks that there must be a "space of appearance" for the actor for politics to come into being.[9] But what she did not imagine is that it might be a space of appearance for the abiding requirements of the body itself. The body that appears is not only comported toward speech but to showing what is required in order to survive, to work, and to live. In the recent public assemblies of those who call themselves "the people," attention is brought to bear on the basic needs of bodily survival, for survival is surely a precondition for all the other claims we make. Survival is a precondition of politics, but not its aim. We survive precisely in order to live, and life, as much as it requires survival, must be *more* than survival in order to be livable.[10] So a demand that follows from this basic condition is precisely for a livable life—not so much equally livable (where equality and livability are reconciled). How, then, do we think about a livable life without positing a single or uniform ideal for that life? It is not a matter, in my view, of finding out what the human really is, or should be, since it has surely been made plain that humans are animals, too, and that their very bodily existence depends upon systems of support that are both human and nonhuman. So to a certain extent, I follow my colleague Donna Haraway in thinking about the complex relationalities that constitute bodily life and suggest that we surely do not need any more ideal forms of the human but rather more complex ways of understanding that set of corporeal relations and interdependencies without which we do not exist at all.[11]

The body is not only a discrete entity with fixed boundaries; it is also a set of relations to food, shelter, sexuality, appearance, mobility, audibility, and visuality. One that is embedded in, or disembedded from, a set of social relations and institutional forms that determine in part whether a bodily life will persist. One body does not really exist without another, and the "dyad" implied by the framework of self and Other cannot do justice to the plurality of bodies that constitute the people. How, finally, do we understand this embodied people, whose vulnerability and agency are conditioned by their environment, technology, sociality, and access to power?

Although there are those who will say that active bodies assembled on the street constitute a powerful and surging multitude, one that in itself constitutes a radical democratic event or action, I can only partially agree with that view. When the people break off from established power, they enact the popular will, though to know that for certain, we would have to know who is breaking off, and where, and who does not break off, and where are they. There are, after all, all sorts of surging multitudes I would not want to endorse (even if I do not dispute their right to assemble), and they would include racist or fascist congregations and violent forms of anti-parliamentary mass movements. I am less concerned with the vitality of surging multitudes or any nascent and promising life-force that seems to belong to their collective action than with joining a struggle to establish more sustaining conditions of livability in the face of increasing precarity. The final aim of politics is not simply to surge forth together (though this can be an essential moment of affective intensity within a broader struggle against precarity), constituting a new sense of the "people" even if sometimes, for the purposes of radical democratic change—which I do endorse—it is important to surge forth in ways that claim and alter the attention of the world for some more enduring possibility of livable life for all.

After all, something has to hold such a group together, some demand, some felt sense of injustice and unlivability, some shared intimation of the possibility of change, and that change has to be fueled by a resistance to, minimally, existing and expanding inequalities, ever-increasing conditions of precarity for many populations, both locally and globally, forms of authoritarian and securitarian control that seek to suppress democratic processes and mass movements. On the one hand, there are bodies that assemble on the street or online or through other less visible networks of solidarity, especially in prisons, whose political claims are made through forms of solidarity that may or may not appear directly in public space; on the other hand, there are mobilizations that emerge in public that make their claims through language, action, gesture, and movement, through linking arms, through refusing to move, to forming bodily modes of obstruction to police and state authorities. A given movement can move in and out of the space of heightened exposure, depending upon its strategies and the military and police threats it must face. In each of these cases, however, we can say that these bodies form networks of resistance together, remembering that bodies are not just active agents of resistance but also fundamentally in need of support. Equally, they are not just in need of support but also capable of resistance. To think politics in this sense is to think through this plural predicament of requiring and demanding support for bodily vulnerability and this mobilization of bodies in the plural in the practices of resistance.

When such movements work, they themselves provide *provisional* support to facilitate the broader demand for forms of *enduring* support that make lives livable. The demand is at once enacted and made, exemplified and communicated. Bodies assemble precisely to show that they are bodies, and to let it be known politically what it means to persist as a body in this world, and what requirements must be met for bodies to survive, and what conditions make a bodily life, which is the only life we have, finally livable.

It is not, then, exclusively or primarily as subjects bearing abstract rights that we take to the streets. If we bear those rights to freedom of assembly, to constitute ourselves as a people, then we enact them in our bodily practices. They may well be stated, but the "statement" is already in the assembly, signified by plural bodies coming together, before anyone has to speak. We take to the streets because we need to walk or move there; we need streets to be structured so that, whether or not we are in a chair, we can move there, and we can pass through that space without obstruction, harassment, administrative detention, or fear of injury or death. If we are on the streets, it is because we are bodies that require infrastructural support for our continuing existence, and for living a life that matters. Mobility is itself a right of the body, to be sure, but also a precondition for the exercise of other rights, including the right of assembly itself. Assembly is at once the condition of any possible claim at the same time that it is a specific right to which an assembly lays claim. That circularity is less a contradiction than a founding condition of a political plurality, a people.

If the body were by definition active—always self-constituting, never constituted—then we would not need to struggle for the conditions that allow the body its free activity in the name of social and economic justice. That struggle presumes that bodies are constrained and constrainable. The condition of bodily vulnerability is brought out into the open in those public assemblies and coalitions that seek to counter accelerating precarity. So it becomes all the more imperative to understand the relation between vulnerability and those forms of activity that mark our survival, our flourishing, and our political resistance. Indeed, even in the moment of actively appearing on the street, we are exposed, vulnerable to injury of one kind or another. This is especially true for those who appear on the street without permits, who are opposing the police or the military or other security forces without weapons, who are transgendered in transphobic environments, who are without documents in countries that criminalize those who seek rights of citizenship. Although one may be shorn of protection, to be sure, one is not reduced to some sort of "bare life." On the contrary, to be shorn of protection is a form of political exposure, at once concretely vulnerable, even breakable, and potentially and actively defiant, even revolutionary. The bodies that assemble designate and form themselves together as "we, the people," targeting those forms of abstraction that would cast bodily requirements once again into oblivion. To show up is both to be exposed and to be defiant, meaning precisely that we are crafted precisely in that disjuncture, and that in crafting ourselves, we expose the bodies for which we make our demand. We do this for and with one another, without any necessary presumption of harmony or love. As a way of making a new body politic.

4

TO RENDER SENSIBLE

GEORGES DIDI-HUBERMAN

Representable People, Imaginary People?

Representation of the people comes up against a double difficulty, if not a double aporia, that comes from the impossibility of our sub-suming each of the two terms, "representation" and "people," into the unity of one concept. Hannah Arendt said that we will never manage to think about the political dimension as long as we stub-bornly persist in speaking of *man*, since politics is interested precisely in something else, which is *men*, whose multiplicity is modulated dif-ferently each time, whether it be in conflict or community.[1] Likewise we must say, and forcefully, that we will never manage to think about the aesthetic dimension—or the world of the "sensible" to which we are reacting at every moment—as long as we speak of *the representa-tion* or *the image*: there are only *images*, images whose very multiplicity, whether it be in conflict or connivance, resists any synthesis.

65

That is why we can say that *the people*, quite simply—"the people" as a unity, identity, totality, or generality—that it quite simply does not exist. Supposing there was still a fully autochthonous population somewhere—as we see, but it is no doubt one of the last known examples, in the documentary images of *First Contact* where the first exchanges, in 1930, were recorded between a group of adventurers and a New Guinea population cut off from the rest of the world since the dawn of time[2]—"the people" do not exist because even in such a case of isolation, the term assumes a minimum of complexity, of impurity represented by the heterogeneous composition of those multiple and various peoples that are the living and their dead, the bodies and their spirits, those of the clan and the others, the males and the females, the humans and their gods or even their animals. . . . There is not *a people*; there are only coexistent *peoples*, not only from one population to another but even within—the social or mental interior of—the same population, no matter how coherent we would like to imagine it to be, which, moreover, is never the case.[3] It is always possible to hypostatize "the people" into *identity* or even into *generality*. But the first is a sham, devoted to glorifying populisms of all kinds, while the second is not to be found, a central aporia for all the "political" or historical sciences.[4]

It is not surprising that Pierre Rosanvallon entitled his historical inquiry on democratic representation in France *Le Peuple introuvable*. From the very beginning of this book appears "malaise," spelled out: the malaise of a democracy—that is, literally, the "power of the people"—extended between the obviousness of its horizon as "political good" and the glaring, often scandalous, incompletion of its reality as "political disappointment." It is very interesting, moreover, that this malaise or this part of "obscurity" inherent to our democratic history then comes back to the question of *representation* as the most necessary but also the thorniest paradigm: "It is around the question of representation, in its two senses as *mandate* and as *figuration*, that the difficulties take shape." But it seems odd—even disturbing—that Pierre

Rosanvallon, whose subject is democracy, only evokes this dialectic of representation through an immediate reference to Carl Schmitt, for whom political representation as *Repräsentation* or "symbolic figuration" must indeed be distinguished from political representation as *Stellvertretung* or "mandate."[5]

We know that in his nostalgia for monarchic power, Carl Schmitt could only play symbolic figuration against democratic mandate. In his *Verfassungslehre* of 1928—one of his fundamental works—Carl Schmitt does not fail to specify that representation

> is not possible with just any type of being, and it presupposes a special [exceptional] type of being (*eine besondere Art Sein*). Something dead, of lesser or no value, or vile (*etwas Totes, etwas Minderwertiges oder Wertloses, etwas Niedriges*) cannot be represented. It lacks that superior type of being (*gesteigerte Art Sein*) that is capable of being elevated to public being, of having an existence (*Existenz*). Words like grandeur, eminence, majesty, glory, dignity and honor attempt to convey that specialness [or exceptionality] (*Besonderheit*) of an elevated being capable of being represented.[6]

From that angle, we cannot see how "the people" or "the peoples" could be in any way *representable*. Carl Schmitt, we know, wanted to unify the notion of the people in its very negativity and powerlessness; for him, the people *is not*. It is not this (not a magistracy or an administration, for example); it is not that (not a political actor in the full sense, for example); all that it knows how to do, according to him, is acclaim the *representation of power* that is presented to it as *Führertum*, as supreme "guidance."[7] Pierre Rosanvallon obviously restrains himself from the extremes of loathing displayed by Carl Schmitt toward "democratic obviousness."[8] But he find himself prisoner of the disjunctive model established by the author of *Political Theology* between *Stellvertretung* and *Repräsentation*. He no doubt inverts the hierarchy— mandate taking precedence henceforth over symbol—but this is once again to play the representation of the peoples against themselves. It is as if, *figured*, the peoples necessarily became *imaginary*; as if, vowed to the image, they inevitably became illusory.

Three "imaginary peoples" thus appear in the eyes of Pierre Rosanvallon: the *opinion-people*, when public opinion is defined as that "inorganic way by which a people makes known what it wants and what it thinks" (according to Hegel) or as the "modern form of acclamation" (according to Carl Schmitt, once again); the *nation-people* that is obsessed with the "populist celebration" to the point of making it an operator of exclusion of everyone from the barbarian to the immigrant; and finally the *emotion-people*, where "the modern masses' quest for identity" is expressed "in a pathetic mode. Lacking in content, these communities of emotion weave no solid bonds. They only bring about fleeting ties and involve no obligations between men. Nor do they involve any future. Far from embodying any promise for change or power for action, as the *event-people* of the Revolution did in the past, the *emotion-people* is not inscribed in history. It is only the fleeting shadow of a lack and a difficulty."[9]

No doubt Pierre Rosanvallon's targets here are above all the "stadiums," the "television screens," and the "magazine columns."[10] But his very expression, the "emotion-people," committed as it is to so harsh a diagnosis, is not without consequences for the two notions it combines, that of the *people* and that of *emotion*, through that third notion, which is, precisely, *representation.* Of course we understand that representation can serve as a vehicle for the artificial emotions of the television screens and the magazine columns; it can even serve, undoubtedly, as a vehicle for the great totalitarian "guidances" to which Carl Schmitt subscribed in 1933. But representation is precisely like the people: it is something multiple, heterogeneous, and complex. Representation—and we know this a little more precisely since Nietzsche and Warburg—brings with it antagonistic or paradoxical structural effects, which could be called "syncopes" on the level at which they function semiotically, or symptomal "rips" on the metapsychological or anthropological level.[11] Thus the *peoples* and their *emotions* ask much more of us than this condescending critique that amounts to dismissal: a philosophically convenient dismissal—essentially Platonic—of the perceptible world in general, of its own *motions* and thus of its possible *resources*.

Rubbing One's Eyes Before the Dialectical Images

Thus we must return a little less haughtily—a little less scornfully—to what Hegel called, with regard to the people, that "inorganic way of making known what it wants and what it thinks," or to what Carl Schmitt conceded to the masses under the category of "acclamation" (obviously Carl Schmitt would have spoken much less of the peoples' protest, their "demonstrations" or their calls for emancipation). If the *emotion-people* is an imaginary people, as Pierre Rosanvallon maintains, that nevertheless does not mean that it would be "lacking in content," "without any solid bonds," doomed to "fleeting ties," and "involving no future [or any] power for action." It only means that it "is not inscribed in history"—and the simplest reason for that is that that *emotions themselves, like images, are inscriptions of history*, its crystals of legibility (*Lesbarkeit*), to adopt here a notion common to a whole constellation of thinkers who were reconsidering the fundamental relationships between historicity and visibility of bodies in the third and fourth decades of the twentieth century, that is to say in a context of struggles against fascism (I am thinking of course of Walter Benjamin, Aby Warburg, Carl Einstein, Ernst Bloch, Siegfried Kracauer, even Theodor Adorno).[12]

Because the emotions themselves—like images, according to the brilliant concept framed by Walter Benjamin—are *dialectical*. That means first of all that they maintain a very specific relationship with representations: a relationship of inherence and disjunction at the same time, a relationship of expression and conflict at the same time. At the very moment when Aby Warburg began to observe the play of "polarizations" and "depolarizations" in "formulas of *pathos*" over the long duration of images,[13] Sigmund Freud was insisting, in his *Traumdeutung*, on a major point that he had already recognized in observing symptoms of hysteria: that the existence of the unconscious implies that a complex dialectic exists—here expression and there conflict, here congruence and there discordance—between *affects* and *representations*.[14] If it is true that the history of societies depends upon the unconscious as well, then we must to bow to the evidence formulated by Walter Benjamin in his *Passagenwerk*: "In the dialectical image, the Past . . . can only be revealed as such at a very specific period: the one in which humanity, rubbing its eyes, perceives precisely as such this dream image (*Traumbild*). It is at that moment that the historian assumes, for that image, the task of interpreting dreams (*die Aufgabe der Traumdeutung*)."[15]

When humanity does not rub its eyes—when its images, its emotions, and its political acts find themselves divided by nothing—then the images are not dialectical, the emotions are "lacking in content," and the political acts themselves "involve no future." What makes the people "not to be found" is thus to be sought in the crisis of their figuration, as well as that of their mandate. That is what Walter Benjamin understood perfectly clearly in his 1935 essay "The Work of Art in the Age of Mechanical Reproduction." "The crisis of democracies," he wrote, "can be understood as a crisis of the conditions of exposure of the political man." There, where "the champion, the star, and the dictator emerge as victors" in the stadiums or on the screens of commercial cinema, it would thus be necessary to *dialecticize the visible*.[16] That is, to make other images, other montages; to look at them differently; to introduce into them division and movement combined, emotion and thought combined. In short, to rub one's eyes, to rub the representation with the affect, the ideal with the repressed, the sublimated with the symptomal.

A *representation of the peoples* becomes possible again beginning from the moment we agree to introduce the dialectical division into the *representation of powers*. It is not sufficient to do as Pierre Rosanvallon does and retrace the history of the political mandate beginning from the democratic premises of Tocqueville; nor is it sufficient to do what Giorgio Agamben does and rethink the archaeology of "reign" and "glory" beginning first with the theological premises of the church fathers, and then with the anti-democratic premises of Carl Schmitt. On the contrary, for Walter Benjamin, to dialecticize consisted of making appear in each fragment of history that "image" that "passes into a flash of lightning," that "arises and vanishes at the moment when it reveals itself to knowledge," but that, in its very fragility, engages the memory and the desire of the peoples, that is to say, the configuration of an emancipated future.[17] This is a way of admitting that in such a domain, the historian must know how to turn his gaze to the least "passing things" or fragilities that, counter to the "sense of history"—in which our "current events" wants so much to believe—arise as if they were coming from very far away and immediately vanish, like signals bearing a historicity unconceived of until then.

Those signals or "dialectical images" are of course fragile. Such is the fragility of the collective emotions as well, and that is nevertheless their great dialectical resource. "On the evening of the first day of fighting [during the Revolution of July 1830]," Benjamin reminds us, "in many places in Paris, at the same moment and without consulting one another, men were seen firing at the clocks." Wasn't that a way, a very "affective" way no doubt, of making "homogeneous and empty time" explode, and of replacing it, through this interposed signal, with a model of "materialist historiography" characterized by the dismantling and rewinding of all temporality?[18] Such is, in any case, the fragility of the peoples themselves; the destruction of some public clocks and the death of some eight hundred July insurgents would not prevent the bourgeois and monarchist take-over of the movement. But Walter Benjamin—who was writing these lines at the moment of greatest danger for himself, that is in 1940—would have wanted to conjure this sort of "dream image" in which all the clocks would be shot, to rub his eyes before it, and to reformulate in this very gesture of *awakening* the task of the historian that falls to us still today in sentences that, for a long time now, I have not let myself recopy:

> To do the work of the historian does not mean knowing "how things really happened." It means seizing upon a memory (*sich einer Erinnerung bemächtigen*), just as it arises at the moment of danger (*wie sie im Augenblick einer Gefahr aufblizt*). It is a matter for historical materialism to retain an image of the past (*ein Bild der Vergangenheit*) that reveals itself unexpectedly to the historical subject at the moment of danger. This danger threatens the contents of the tradition as much as its addressees. It is the same for them both, and consists for them of being made the instrument of the dominant class. In each period, it is necessary to seek to wrench the tradition once again from the conformism that is on the verge of subjugating it.[19]

This insistence on the "tradition"—as distinguished from all cultural "conformism"—ought not to surprise us in a context nevertheless dominated by immediate danger and the urgency of responding to it politically. Benjamin shared with Freud and Warburg the acute awareness of the *anthropological effectiveness of relics*; he shared with Bataille and Eisenstein the cheerful perception of a *political effectiveness of relics*, which came of rubbing one's eyes before the animal carcasses at the Villette slaughterhouses or before the skeletons moving in a Mexican procession, and as later filmmakers such as Jean Rouch, Pier Paolo Pasolini, or Glauber Rocha had to show with perfect clarity. But that historical perception—and transhistorical as well, since it grants a decisive place to the long durations and to the *missing links*, to the heterochronies and to the returns of the repressed—depended upon the *division* that supports and sustains any representation of the peoples. Where Carl Schmitt was only interested in the *tradition of power*, Benjamin firmly opposes to it the *tradition of the oppressed*: "The tradition of the oppressed teaches us that the 'state of exception' in which we live is the rule. We must achieve a conception of history that is aware of this situation."[20]

We understand better that Walter Benjamin was at the same time locating the task of the historian—and no doubt of the artist as well—through his desire to *make the peoples represented*, that is to say to give a worthy representation to the "nameless" of history: "It is more difficult to honor the memory of the nameless (*das Gedächtnis der Namenlosen*) than the memory of the recognized [*passage crossed out*: celebrated, the poets and thinkers are not an exception]. The construction of history is dedicated to the memory of the nameless."[21] This task is all at once *philological*—or "micrological" as Benjamin liked to say—and *philosophical*. It requires exploring the archives into which the "conformists" of history never stick their noses (or open their eyes); at the same time it requires a "theoretical framework" (*theoretische Armatur*) and a "constructive principle" (*konstructiv Prinzip*) that positivist history lacks completely.[22]

This "theoretical framework" presupposes not pledging the allegiance of images to ideas, or ideas to facts. When, for example, Benjamin speaks of the "tradition of the oppressed" (*Tradition der Unterdrückten*), he is no doubt using a Marxist vocabulary referring directly to the class struggle, but he knows just as well that the word *Unterdrückung* is part of the conceptual vocabulary of Freudian psychoanalysis. Translated into French as *répression*, it designates a type of psychological process for which *refoulement* (*Verdrängung*) appears as a particular subcategory. *Répression* can be conscious, while *refoulement* is always unconscious; *répression* can be applied to affects, while *refoulement* operates only on representations.[23] Thus it falls to the historian to render the peoples "representable" by making represented exactly that which is found to be "repressed" in their traditional or, more accurately, conformist representations. Now, what is "repressed" in such representations involves not only their status of social invisibility—what Hannah Arendt wanted to examine, for example, in *The Jew as Pariah: A Hidden Tradition*, through the figure of the pariah—but once again what Hegel called the "inorganic way by which a people makes known what it wants and what it thinks" by expressing affects through the intermediary of gestures of the body and motions of the soul.[24]

Lifting the Lid, Making the Heterotopias Visible

The best historians are those who contribute most effectively to lifting the lid—the lid of the repression, of the *Unterdrückung*, of the peoples. It is not part of my intention here, of course, to offer a litany of the masterpieces of the discipline of history, from Burckhardt and Michelet to contemporary writings. But I would like to mention briefly three oeuvres thanks to which, it seems to me in an exemplary fashion, the lid was not only lifted but smashed to pieces. The first is that of Michel de Certeau: beginning with a *history of solitudes*—mystical solitudes in particular—Michel de Certeau touched upon the "absent" in conventional history and went so far as to explore the acts of *social resistance* inherent to certain "arts of living" among the most "ordinary" people.[25]

As for Michel Foucault, he began, as we know, with a *history of deviances* and their institutional treatments: psychological deviances and the asylum, somatic deviances and the clinic, criminal deviances and the prison, sexual and indeed even literary deviances (in the work of Raymond Roussel, for example).[26] Whereas he also finished, according to his archivist (that is to say philological) inquiries equipped with a critical (that is to say philosophical) framework and "constructive principle," by distinguishing certain places where such a "tradition of the oppressed" could be recognized, assembled, organized, united. These places he called *heterotopias*. Not that such places can exist as the functional settings of a fully guaranteed liberty:

> I do not believe in the existence of something that would be functionally—by its true nature—radically liberating. Liberty is a practice. Thus there can exist, in fact, a certain number of projects that aim at altering certain constraints, at making them more flexible or even at breaking them, but none of those projects can, simply by its nature, guarantee that people will automatically be free, human freedom is never ensured by the institutions and the laws whose function it is to guarantee it. . . . If one found a place—and perhaps it exists—where liberty is effectively exercise, one would discover that that is not thanks to the nature of the objects, but once again, thanks to the practice of freedom. Which does not mean that after all one can also just leave people in slums, thinking that they only have to exercise their rights. . . . There are not, by definition, machines of freedom. . . . There are only reciprocal relationships, and constant gaps between them.[27]

Heterotopias define the very space of these possible gaps—where the lid trembles, moves a little, and lets escape the scalding steam of freedom. Utopias function perfectly, but in an unreal way—and a comforting way, adds Foucault elsewhere—whereas heterotopias function in a very real way, although at the price of functioning in a shaky, patched together, imperfect, never complete way. Heterotopias bring into play "a space of dispute both mythical and real in the space where we live," says Foucault. They have "the power to juxtapose in a single real place many spaces, many locations that are in themselves incompatible," indeed even many heterogeneous temporalities (one would say in this sense that archives, museums, and libraries are, in Michel Foucault's eyes, heterotopias hidden beneath their own institutional paneling). As such they appear as a "great reserve of imagination," and it is up to us to make liberal use of them.[28]

It is on this school of freedom that Arlette Farge would also draw for book after book with elegance and obstinacy. For her, the archives would be the almost unhoped-for—but immediately inexhaustible—opportunity for lifting the lid that the archivists themselves no doubt believed to be irremovable.[29] She laid claim to a sensation, which is also a methodological principle, well described in the past by Aby Warburg at the time of his tireless explorations into the *ricordanze* of the Florentine archive of the Renaissance: "The voices of the deceased echo still in the hundreds of deciphered archival documents, and in the thousands of others that are not yet deciphered; the historian's devotion can restore the timbre of those inaudible voices (*historische Pietät vermag der unhörbaren Stimmen weider Klangfarbe zu verleihen*), if he does not shrink from effort of restoring the natural link between word and image (*die natürliche Zusammengehörigkeit von Wort und Bild*)."[30]

It is equipped with this kind of methodical intuition that a history of the peoples could commence or recommence. Arlette Farge renewed one of Karl Marx's gestures—his legal defense of those who stole wood in 1842—by working first on the food thefts in eighteenth-century Paris.[31] She has renewed Benjamin's injunction regarding the "tradition of the oppressed" by dedicating a large portion of her work to the Parisian street peoples, but also to the heterogeneous dimensions that are, on the one hand, "public opinion" and, on the other, "writing of oneself" or "on oneself."[32] She has accompanied and extended the work of Michel Foucault by interrogating the "fragile life" of the poor, the marginal, and the oppressed.[33] In doing so, she has lifted the lid of the discourse generally held over—that is to say hanging over—social conditions and allowed to escape in the *representation* of the peoples, their *symptoms* and their *affects*, what she has described so well in her book *Effusion et tourment*, whose preamble ventures this impossible feat:

It is the breath of the anonymous and hardly well-off bodies of the eighteenth century that will be retranscribed here, those that think and shake themselves, are charmed, disturbed, become violent.

There exist in the most destitute bodies (as in those of others) the will and the dream of multiple escapes, the invention of gestures created or hinted at for them to succeed and words to name them, thus to appropriate them. The mute physical and bodily power of the anonymous, activated by the hope of the future and easily remembering what was, encounters power, responds to it, and speaks with it to be integrated into it or to alter it. . . .

Something shivers there. The bodies hum and elaborate their fates. Men and women, beings of the flesh, are "affectively in the world." They struggle constantly against their own bodies and are in inevitable symbiosis with them, in order to banish not only cold, hunger, and fatigue but also injustice, hatred, and violence. Activated by history and acting upon it, they are ordinary beings. . . . This is a long way from wanting to define (as was often done) the weakest ones solely by the primary needs and desires of their bodies, which have elsewhere been called uncultivated. On the contrary, attempting to approach historically and politically the "material part of animate beings" [the usual definition of the body] confirms the body's infinite nobility, its rational and passionate ability to create *with* history and *despite* it, since it is the seat of and party to sensations, feelings, and perceptions. Ductile, it includes itself in the world as much as that is possible for it. The price is laughter and cries, gestures and loves, blood and sorrows, fatigue as well. The body, its history, and history itself make up only one thing.[34]

To say, first of all, that bodies—bodies singular and multiple, not "the body" in general—are "activated by history and act upon it" is to adopt a *historical position* that was inaugurated by Jacob Burkhardt, defended by Nietzsche, and confirmed by Warburg, as well as by Marc Bloch and a number of great ethnologists and sociologists: a position according to which history is not recounted solely through a sequence of human *actions* but also through an entire constellation of *passions* and emotions felt by the peoples. To say next that bodies are "affectively in the world" is to assume a *philosophical position* informed by the phenomenology of the sensible that is found in an exemplary way in Erwin Straus, Jean-Paul Sartre, or Maurice Merleau-Ponty. It is to open history to a whole anthropology of affected bodies, affective bodies.[35] To say finally that "something shivers there" is to enter into a *literary position*, since to write history so well is first of all to write; this engages the historian in formal, stylistic, narrative, and even poetic choices, choices that determine the content as well as the style of one's production of knowledge.

These three stances act indissociably in each attempt to give the peoples a worthy historical representation. We find them, for example, in the works of Jacques Rancière, where the *historical position* is conveyed through his work on the archives of the peoples—a modesty very rare in the practices of the philosophical community to which Rancière belongs first—as seen for instance in the collection assembled in collaboration with Alain Faure on *La Parole ouvrière*, as well as the large book of archives entitled *La Nuit des prolétaires*.[36] Now this choice of method very much involves a *literary position* characterized by a concern for material detail and a respect for documents and their concomitant editing. To do this, Rancière would draw on the sources of French realism of the nineteenth century, from the "micrologies" of Gustave Flaubert (this exact contemporary of Karl Marx) to the *Carnets d'enquêtes* of Émile Zola, or from the texts of Michelet to the Paris writings of Rainer Maria Rilke.[37] He would only lack, in all these ventures in historical immanence, the audacity of a supplementary operation, precisely the one that a Walter Benjamin or a Georges Bataille knew how to put to work—with the help of Proustian memoire, surrealist encounter, or Freudian metapsychology—in each historical document by detecting in it a symptomal enactment requiring of the historian that "task of interpreting dreams" of which the *Passagenwerk* speaks.[38]

Jacques Rancière has nonetheless lifted a few heavy "lids" off historicist conformism, guided in that by a *philosophical position* that owes much to the reading of Karl Marx most certainly, but also in a quieter way—and perhaps by way of that other great political philosopher in France, Claude Lefort[39]—by all that, in the work of Maurice Merleau-Ponty, could render evident the points of contact between the *dialectical*, from which would proceed a philosophy of history, and the *sensible*, upon which is founded all phenomenology of the body.[40] Isn't thinking about the relationships between the political and the aesthetic from the angle of an "allotment of the sensible," as Jacques Rancière does, in effect rediscovering the dialectical operations of the work in that "domain of the sensible" that so many aesthetes would like to imagine pure of all conflictuality and all negativity?[41] By the same token, don't we need to recognize in any political *demonstration*—this word may be understood more concretely or more philosophically as one pleases—the very encounter of a dialectical relationship and a sensible relationship, as these lines by Rancière on the distinction between the *political* and the *police* clearly remind us:

> "Move on! There's nothing to see." The police says that there's nothing to see on a road, nothing to do but keep moving. Says that the space of traffic is only the space of traffic. The political consists of transforming that traffic space into a demonstration space of a subject: the people, the workers, the citizens. It consists of refiguring the space, what there is to do there, to see there, to name there. It is the litigation introduced over the allotment of the sensible. . . . The essence of the political is dissensus. Dissensus is not the confrontation of interests or opinions. It is the demonstration of a gap in the sensible itself. The political demonstration makes visible what had no reasons for being seen, it lodges one world within another, for example the world where the factory is a public place within the one where it is a private place, the world where the workers speak, and speak of the community, within the one in which they cry out to express their single pain.[42]

Thus the demonstration is what happens when citizens declare themselves oppressed by daring to declare their powerlessness, their pain, and their concomitant emotions. It is what happens when a *sensible* event touches the community in its history, that is to say, in the *dialectic* of its evolving. Thus the *affective* and the *effective* are deployed in it together. Where Alain Badiou wanted to postulate a sense of history in which this concomitance would be "saturated, terminated" and would have to give way to a "nonexpressive conception of the philosophical dialectic," we can, on the contrary, observe everywhere the survival and effectiveness of the very oldest "formulas of *pathos*": lamentations that rise and become imprecations, screamed curses that become actions. There is no "politics of the truth" as Badiou says—qualifying it as "real and logical" to better disqualify, in an entirely Platonic fashion, what would be on the order of the imaginary or the emotional—without the *truth of the sensible*.[43] At the very moment when I write these lines (June 2012), all that Eisenstein put into images in the scenes of lamentations in *Battleship Potemkin* is finding a new value of urgency in the concomitance of *tears* shed at all the funerals of the victims of the Syrian regime of Bachar el-Assad, the *cries* hurled in the face of the police, and the *arms* that it is becoming necessary to procure to ensure a future—now that it is impossible to have dialogue—to such protest.

Approaching, Documenting, Rendering Sensible

To approach politics through the multiple opportunities of a "litigation introduced over the allotment of the sensible," as Jacques Rancière would have it: isn't this to end up by "aestheticizing the political"—the worst thing in the eyes of Walter Benjamin (because that was what the fascist regimes of his time did, with great pomp), something for which we can, in any case, occasionally reproach the author of *Partage du sensible?* The answer to this question is very simple: it is that aesthetics itself designates a field of conflicts, a division that many other words have crossed over, for example when we want to hear in the word *people* (the famous, the overrepresented in the glitter market) all those from which the *peoples* are, rightly, excluded; or when we want to hear in the word *image* (the medium for fame, for overrepresentation in glitter) all that the *images* know, rightly, to contest. What is the meaning then of the word *aesthetic* when Jacques Rancière does not hesitate to write that "the emancipation of workers was first of all an aesthetic revolution: the gap opened in relationship to the sensible universe 'imposed' by a condition"?[44]

We are a long way here from the aesthetic that chooses for its subjects the "criteria of art" or of beauty—what Carl Einstein denounces as the ridiculous "beauty contests"—dear to academic institutions. The aesthetic we are talking about from now on is a kind of knowledge that chooses for subjects the *events of the sensible*, regardless of whether or not they are "artistic." Now, to better describe them, we need not only that philosophical *criticism* developed by Jacques Rancière, among others, but also a true *anthropology* that would benefit from being informed by the "techniques of the body" (according to the lesson of Marcel Mauss), the "formulas of *pathos*" (according to the lesson of Aby Warburg), or the "*thymic* moments" (according to the lesson of phenomenological descriptions, like those of Ludwig Binswanger for example). But in order to describe, one must first know how to write, that is, to take a position—literary, aesthetic, ethical—in the language, that vast field of conflicts where the most reductive and most open usages are encountered, the worst slogans and the best questionings. An anthropology of sensible events begins from the moment when one agrees to *approach* through looking, through listening, through writing, even if it means renouncing the apodictic claims of the metaphysics of school:

> Classical metaphysics was able to pass through a specialty where only literature had done so because it functioned on a basis of undisputed rationalism and because it was convinced of being able

to make the world and human life understood through an organization of concepts. . . . That all changed when phenomenological or existential philosophy chose for its task not to explain the world or to discover its "conditions of possibility" but to formulate an experience of the world, a contact with the world that precedes all thinking *about* the world. . . . From then on the task of literature and the task of philosophy could no longer be separated. When it is a matter of articulating the experience of the world and of showing how consciousness escapes into the world, we can no longer profess to achieve a perfect transparency of expression. Philosophical expression assumes the same ambiguities as literary expression, if the world is made in such a way that it can only be expressed in "stories" and pointed to with the finger.[45]

In order to speak as I do of this "dialectic of the sensible," I do not know if Jacques Rancière would accept such a philosophical intervention (intervention from a phenomenological perspective in Merleau-Ponty's sense, or even from an anthropological perspective in Mauss's sense, revisited by Georges Bataille). But it is clear that, right up to his recent work, *Aisthesis*, Rancière often proceeds by "scenes" that are so many singular "stories" or objects "pointed to with the finger" according to the characteristic gesture of an *approach* that is as descriptive as it is problematized.[46] If the last chapter of this book is devoted to James Agee and his extraordinary study of impoverished Alabama in the 1930s, it is obvious that the philosophical position claimed here is inseparable from a literary position meant to approach sensible phenomena (as a philologist or a historian could do before a document, as an ethnologist would do before a ritual gesture) as much as to discern in them the force lines or the front lines (as a philosopher of the dialectic could do before any given situation).[47]

This literary position has a long history henceforth, Walter Benjamin and Ernst Bloch having known better than anyone in the 1930s how to understand the full political as well as poetic scope of it: from Louis Aragon's *Le Paysan de Paris* and André Breton's *Nadja* to Alfred Döblin's *Alexanderplatz*, from Brechtian montages to the scenaristic writing of Moholy-Nagy, from Blaise Cendrars, Ilya Ehrenburg, or Vladimir Mayakovsky—I am thinking for example of the extraordinary "poem-reports" of 1925–1929[48]—it is all a literary constellation that, beyond the novelistic writings of the nineteenth century, would seek to adopt the principle of *documentary montage* that we find later in the works of W. G. Sebald, Charles Reznikoff, or closer to us, Jean-Christophe Bailly.[49]

Now this principle of documentary montage—or remontage—is inseparable from a cultural history profoundly marked, prior to the cinema, by a certain use of photography.[50] That was how the *dialectic* encountered the *sensible* and how the political was embodied in the new resources, including visual ones, of poetry. In 1924, for example, Blaise Cendrars published a book entitled *Kodak (documentaire)*; the American firm having in the meantime asserted its rights, Cendrars had to reduce his title for the complete edition of his poems in 1944 to simply *Documentaires*.[51] In 1928, this principle entered into the very poetics of the dreamy, amorous course of *Nadja*, the text of which was punctuated by the urban photographs of Jacques-André Boiffard and Man Ray.[52] It was also necessary that the enterprise of theoretical demontage conducted by Georges Bataille in the journal *Documents* in 1929–1930 was not illustrated but very much supported and required by the documentary iconography of Boiffard himself, of Eli Lotar, and of many others as well.[53] In those same years, the *sensible* images of Germaine Krull came again to require the *dialectical* thinking of Walter Benjamin on the Paris arcades (we can rediscover some of those images in the archives of another great dialectician, Theodor Adorno).[54] When Ilya Ehrenburg published his book *Mon Paris* in Moscow in 1933, he had his Leica photographed by El Lissitzky—who was also the book's designer—first facing forward with himself in profile, then immediately photographed close up, a way of saying that perhaps the Leica was the main author of this book composed of an admirable series of images showing the diverse peoples of Paris.[55] And finally—to cut short this list that could go on very much longer—how are we to understand Bertolt Brecht's *Work Journals* or *ABC of the War* without their photographic montages, or James Agee's study without Walker Evans's implacable photographs?[56]

Implacable images indeed.[57] But not "insensible" for all that, not in the least, these images that do not leave us insensible either. Of course no one is crying in these images of poverty, in which unemployment, hunger, and death as well lurk everywhere. One wife almost seems to be biting her lower lip precisely in order not to cry; a frantic child, squatting on ground, unable to play, looks into the void; looking carefully, isn't that other baby crying in its mother's arms? Thus in these images there is all possible dereliction and at the same time all remaining dignity in the bond established with the photographer. As with August Sander, nothing was shot hastily, everything results from a shared *consideration*, a mutual respect that took time to be established. And that is how Walker Evans "renders sensible" to us something crucial—and not only apparent—in the condition of the American peoples of the Great Depression, something that remains inseparable from the account James Agee would give of them.

In such a context then, what does the gesture of *rendering sensible* mean? It does not mean to render unintelligible, whether the strict versions of Platonism or of contemporary rationalism like it or not. If Walter Benjamin constructed his whole approach of the "legibility of history" around the notion of *dialectical image*—and not, for example, on those of "dialectical idea," or even "idea of the dialectic"—it is very much because historical and anthropological intelligibility cannot do without a dialectic of images, appearances, apparitions, gestures, looks . . . all that could be called *sensible events*. As for the *power of legibility* for which these events are the bearers, it is effective only because it involves the very effectiveness of images to render accessible, to call up, not only aspects of things or states of phenomena but also their sensible points, their "sore points," as we so accurately say to locate where sensitivity functions to excess, where something may be wrong, where everything divides into the dialectical deployment of memories, desires, and conflicts.

Thus to render sensible is also to render accessible that *dialectic of the symptom* crossing through all history, usually without the knowledge of official observers (I mean, for example, that James Agee and Walker Evans would lay out before us certain aspects of the economic crisis that the economists or historians of that era undoubtedly did not see so precisely). This could be a way of understanding what Maurice Blanchot was saying when he evoked the "presence of the people . . . not as the whole of social forces, ready for particular political decisions, but in its . . . *declaration of powerlessness.*"[58] In such a way that "to render sensible" would mean, strictly speaking, to render sensible the faults, places, or moments through which, declaring themselves "powerless," the peoples affirm both what they lack and what they desire. Walker Evans's images (dry and yet so moving), like James Agee's descriptions (literal and yet so poetic), thus appear as the *rendering sensible* and the *declaration of powerlessness* of those peoples grappling with a historical and political situation that threatens to destroy them.[59]

To render sensible thus would be to render accessible to the senses, even to render accessible what our senses, like our intelligences, do not always know how to perceive as "making sense": something that appears only as a flaw in the meaning, sign, or symptom. But in a third sense, "to render sensible" also means that we ourselves, before these flaws or symptoms, suddenly become "sensible" to something of the life of the peoples—to something of the history—that escaped us until then but that "regards" us directly. Thus, here we are "rendered sensible" or sensitive to something new in the history of the peoples that we desire, consequently, to know, to understand, and to accompany. Here our senses, but also our significative productions on the historical world, are *moved* by this "rendering sensible": moved in the double sense of putting into emotion and putting into movement of thought.

Thus, here we are before the "declaration of powerlessness" of the peoples—as it can be rendered sensible to us in the montages of James Agee's texts and Walker Evans's images—left grappling with a whole world of *dialectical emotions*, as if the legibility of history necessitated that particular affective disposition that seizes us before such dialectical images: the *formula* with the *pathos* that nevertheless divides it, the intelligible with the sensible that nevertheless turns it upside down.

5

THE PEOPLE AND THE THIRD PEOPLE

SADRI KHIARI

You don't have anything to do this Saturday? So go walk around Saint-Denis—line 13 or RER C—and talk to the passers-by. Pick out a French black or Arab and ask him, "What people do you belong to?" If he answers you, "I belong to the French people," you will know that he is a flunky. If he answers you sincerely, he will say to you, "I belong to the black people—or Arab or Berber, Malian, Muslim, Senegalese, Algerian, African. . . ." Then pick out a so-called stock Frenchman and ask him the same question. He won't say to you, "I belong to the white or European or Christian people"; he will answer you, "I am part of the French people." These distinctions could be without great consequence if it were simply a matter of both parties defining one of the identities dear to them, as for example with two Frenchmen, one of whom might be proud of coming from Dunkirk, the other from Marseilles. But to claim to be part of a people is much more than that. It is to establish the group to which one belongs in society and to assert one's privileged relationship to the state, or to be more precise, to the nation-state. If two large segments of the same French population, one a wide majority—

recognized by the state and recognizing itself in it—and the other a minority—not recognized by the state and not recognizing itself in it—have opposing responses, that poses a major strategic problem to one as well as to the other.

Against Whom Are the People Constituted?

The question "What is the people?" must naturally be answered by another question: against whom are the people constituted? Most of the time we wonder what the immanent characteristics of the people are, the "material" elements, the accounts or myths on which the consciousness of the individuals belonging to a single people is based. We proceed in the same way—and wrongly—for the nation. Whereas those elements reputed to constitute the people do not assemble, do not coalesce, do not consider themselves to be an articulated, coherent, indivisible whole, all those elements only metamorphose into potential power for collective mobilization, only make political sense beginning from the moment when an *exterior* to the people, potentially hostile to the people, becomes apparent. In other words, if the elements that in some way constitute the infrastructure of the people are neither contingent nor arbitrary, they are not sufficient in themselves to constitute the people. Those elements only constitute the condition for the possible emergence of the entity of the people. For the latter to be effectively crystallized, that hostile exterior must exist, whether it is a matter of a feudal aristocracy, the neighboring people, the oppressing people, or a segment of the people considered harmful. The people: these are relationships of power, it is a history, a history of power relationships. It is a history through which the notion of people imposes itself on the universal scale. It is the history of colonial and capitalist modernity. To say that is to affirm two things: first, that the notion of people allows the expression of a political form that colonized the whole of social relationships on the planetary scale;

second, that it has a multitude of meanings that reflect the specific contexts in which it is mobilized.

The universe of meaning in which the notion of people is deployed and takes on specific meanings is generally constructed on the articulation, never identical, of three other notions: the nation, citizenship/sovereignty, and the classes that we call subordinate.[1] What can be retained of the plurality of the forms of articulation of these notions is their plasticity, their permeability in relationship to one another, and their capacity to metamorphose or even merge into one another. Each term of this triptych can be absorbed by another or disappear completely. I will offer as an extreme illustration the situation of national liberation movements or so-called national wars, in the course of which the citizenship merges completely with popular sovereignty, which then becomes entangled in turn with national sovereignty. In this case, the interclassist "national union" assimilates, at least in the representation that it makes of itself, all the components of the population into an indissociable people-nation. Alternatively, an intensified class struggle or a revolutionary situation tends to identify the people with the subordinate classes. In that situation, national sovereignty tends to dissolve into popular sovereignty. We can also cite the example of liberation movements that to a greater or lesser degree cover forms of class struggle. The people-nation thus identifies itself with the subordinate categories of the population, while the dominant classes are likened to the foreigner, exteriorized in relationship to the people-nation. To complete this description, we can mention the case in which the people, even while giving itself the same foundations as the nation, self-identifies as "less" than the nation, generally in that even while being attached to certain autonomous powers, particularly on the cultural plane, it does not aspire to (or renounce) granting itself a state that would be its own (we can mention in this regard the many "minority peoples" in the European states).

The notion of people can thus be tied to particular positions in the socioeconomic order. But these are hardly sufficient to give meaning to the notion of people, at the heart of which there is the allocation of political powers and honors, that is to say, statutory distinctions in the modern order of the state. It thus appears that the notion of people is first of all a political notion. And thus it necessarily has a strategic dimension. Power is always to be won or retained against a real or imagined enemy or rival of the people.

The People With or Against the Race

This way of approaching the people remains very much incomplete, however, if we fail to add to the triptych already mentioned a fourth term without which an understanding of power relationships in France would be faulty. I am speaking of race. I maintain that the notion of people, in its modern sense, was constructed in close connection with the social production of races by colonization. In the history of modernity, some peoples were thus *explicitly* affirmed as racial, and until very recent times (in segregationist America, Hitler's Germany, South Africa, and so on). The racial dimension of the notion of people has generally been masked however by the dominant bourgeois universalism and egalitarianism. In the abstract humanist notion of the people, there is in effect no question of races; humanity is one, distributed into peoples-nations and not into races.

To avoid hasty accusations, I would nevertheless like to specify what I mean by "race," or more exactly by "social races," since race is nothing other than the relationship between domination and resistance to oppression that exists between racialized human groups. Sometimes, to better understand things, changing the words is enough. Thus I propose systematically substituting the word "discrimination" for its opposite, "privilege." For some years, it has generally been admitted that in France there exist forms of discriminatory practices tied to skin color, origin, or culture. The law speaks of fighting them, of multiple public and private institutions attempting to evaluate them, to understand the direct or indirect logic of them, and to devise corrective mechanisms. We recognize as well that they involve almost all areas of social life: economic relationships, as much in the private sector as in the public sphere; urban configurations; the law; education; access to housing, culture, and leisure activities; representation in the various means of communication; political participation; presence in institutions; and so on. We similarly acknowledge that certain populations are discrimination's particular victims, populations descended from immigration from the recent decades, natives of the Maghreb or black Africa, and those of the "overseas territories." Finally, we agree in saying that these forms of discrimination are massive and persist from generation to generation. Now let us take a chart or any sort of diagram designed to establish these discriminatory practices and *let us reverse it*. We had, for example, the following facts: "Among those individuals twenty-five to fifty years old, for the whole French population, unemployment is 20 percent. It is 30 percent for those French citizens born of Maghrebian, African, or overseas parentage" (the figures used here are completely arbitrary and the situation described very oversimplified, but it is just to illustrate my remarks). So let us reverse the chart. Now we have this: "Among those individuals twenty-five to fifty years old, for the whole French population, unemployment is 20 percent. It is 10 percent for the French citizens born of parents of so-called French stock, whites, Europeans, Christians." This chart would no longer be a chart involving discriminatory practices but a chart of *privileges*. If we proceed in the same manner in other areas of social life, we will have a clear image of what a racial society is: a society characterized by privileges granted to a category of the population defined or not by an officially recognized status: to be white, Christian, European. And I would add that since this privilege involves access to state power as well, the state plays a key role in permitting the racial system to continue.

"Social races" must thus be understood as the existence of a conflictual hierarchy of powers among social groups that are distinguished by status, spoken or unspoken, that orders human beings according to the criteria of colors and cultures, constructed in the European colonization movement worldwide and perpetuated today in contemporary forms of empire.

In France, no doubt because its national ideology is constructed around the universalizing—and civilizing—mission of the French people, the masking of racial hierarchies is particularly evident. In the period of the empire, the laws of the Republic established a statutory distinction between the "true" French, granted citizenship, and the "indigenous" subjects of the colonies, but the colonial state itself preferred to conceal the racial density of the notion of the French people. Outside of small groups on the extreme right, the same denial persists, as much on the right as within the overwhelming majority on the left. If I write, "the French people is the white French people," I will indeed find myself accused of using the same language as the white-supremacist nationalists. Nevertheless I can do nothing else but write: *the French people is the white French people!* And I will add, to be more precise: of European and Christian origin. The others, those who have not had the luck to be born white, European, and Christian, do and do not belong to the people: they are the *third-people*. That is not to say what a militant neo-Nazi would say but to say what all the French more or less clearly think. Above all, it is to name the reality of power relationships and relationships to the institutions of power of the white, European, Christian majority facing the minority descended from non-European immigration.

One more word. The "republican pact" in which the ideology and the institutions constituting the French people coalesces, solidly formed around democratic citizenship, a certain redistributive social compromise, and national preeminence, was established at the point where many stakes crossed: social and political conflicts within France, competition with other empire states, and colonial expansion.

The French people, the French state, and the French nation are the products of it; that is to say, they were shaped by the power relationships born of colonialization. Today various factors are jeopardizing this structure: liberal and financial globalization, the institutionalization of the European Union, the loss of influence of French imperialism, and the growing presence of a nonwhite population native to the colonies. For some years, one of the reasons, and not the least of them, for the racialist policies of the state, whether led by the right or by the PS [Parti socialiste], has been to reinforce the racial dimension of the republican pact to compensate for the deleterious effects of those factors that undermine it and over which it has only very little control. In the name of the incompatibility between the "values" of the Republic and/or of the "national identity," on the one hand, and the "cultures" and beliefs of the French born of colonial immigration, on the other, in the name of the "necessity" of controlling or interrupting migratory flows, of protecting "French" employment, of fighting terrorism or lax security, the notion of people has been drawn more narrowly around the so-called French stock: white, European, Christian. In other words, this policy seeks to revamp the very sorry state of the notion of French people in the easiest possible way: against the nonwhites. If some of the most nationalist movements put particular emphasis on "stock," other more liberal or more internationalist ones emphasize the reference to a white European "identity," always as opposed to the nonwhites, fundamental to what a European people would supposedly be.[2]

Faced with the crises of the republican pact, but also faced with the racialist offensive of powers that are in the political majority, the radical left is itself struggling hard to find its way.

The National Inflexion of the Radical Left

With the exception perhaps of ecologists and some sympathies on the far left, a certain "sovereignist" discourse is now given voice by all the parties. Within the principal forces present on the electoral scene (the UMP [Union pour un mouvement populaire] and allies, the PS and allies, the FN [Front national]), this rhetoric is paradoxically in accord with the defense of the principal mechanisms for liberal globalization. It cannot be reduced to its demagogic electioneering nature, however; in the case of race, it has a deeper function as well, without ambiguity in its approach to the urban suburbs and immigration.

The majority of the organized powers of the radical left do not themselves escape the revamping of the nationalist paradigm, articulated around the notions of people and popular sovereignty. The most obvious expression of this inclination is undoubtedly the rallying of the "left of the left" around the Left Front and Jean-Luc Mélanchon, dissident of the Socialist Party and allied to the French Communist Party, who developed his antiliberal and nationalist discourse around the theme of "popular sovereignty." In the last presidential election, Jean-Luc Mélanchon obtained 11 percent of the vote thanks to a campaign that could be summed up in two slogans: "Long live the French people" and "The people want the power." During his election campaign, he thus emphasized the sovereignty of which the French people were dispossessed by the liberal reasoning of globalization, international financial institutions, and the Central European Bank. Although he carefully avoided substituting the notion of popular sovereignty with that of national sovereignty, he nevertheless endeavored to promote the principal symbols of French nationalism (the tricolored flag, the *Marseillaise*, the myth of France as the nation of the rights of man and of the universal . . .), constantly referring moreover to the notion of "homeland." Furthermore he indicated his desire to reassert France's national independence, which for him largely converged with restoring its role as an international power, with the expansionist strength of its economy, the exploitation of its immense maritime space and its (colonial) presence throughout the world, the tools of its cultural influence like French-speaking institutions, its military power, and its network of alliances, whose renewal in the direction of "emergent powers" would supposedly allow it to counter its current subordination to the United States.[3] Of course Jean-Luc Mélanchon embraced certain social demands that emphasized his engagement with the left: he opposed the liberal anarchy and unchecked financial globalization with its disastrous effects on the working classes; he denounced as well the expansionism and arrogance of the United States. His plan nevertheless fell within the national-imperialist perspective of constituting a new international pole within which France would play a chief role. It could thus regain its lost splendor. This expresses the equivocal nature of the notion of people as it figures into the discourse of the Mélanchon left. Citizenship and popular sovereignty are strongly linked there with national sovereignty, itself the condition and end of a politics of power. Thus the people does not appear to be synonymous with the subordinate classes but to be the form through which the subordinate classes are joined in solidarity with the imperial Republic, through the rehabilitation of the old republican pact—as it is idealized in any case, that is to say, combining expansion of democratic rights, mechanisms of social redistribution, and nationalism.

That is where Mélanchon's policy toward the populations descended from immigration and working-class neighborhoods finds its coherence. Whereas the political formations backing neoliberalism, incapable of preserving the social systems, tend to reinforce the racial dimension of the old republican pact, Mélanchon's strategy involves the inverse logic consisting of privileging those dimensions of citizenship, redistribution, and nationalism rather than its racial reasoning. Thus even if he does not abandon a certain prudence, no doubt to keep his white constituency happy, he allows himself to defend the democratic and social rights of immigrants and those living in working-class neighborhoods, and in that way he distinguishes himself from the right and from the Socialist Party. At the same time, there is no question for him of tolerating the least calling into question of the "Republic one and indivisible" and its "principles," the inescapable foundations, according to him, of the sovereignty of the people and the national French matrix.

Thus to French blacks, Arabs, and Muslims, Mélanchon can only propose assimilation within the "people one and indivisible," the institutions that constitute it, its dominant culture, its "national" history, and its norms. That is why, to cite only this example, he does not hesitate to deny any relevance to the notion of Islamophobia and to take over the campaign in defense of secularism, that is to say, an instrument of relegation for Islamic populations and of stigmatization for a religion judged to be invasive and threatening to the white, Christian, European French norm. Now such an assimilationist process, as it is carried out against the Muslims or other groups born of colonial immigration, signifies in concrete terms their exclusion outside of the people. In other words, even though its ambition is to represent the whole of the disadvantaged populations in France, the notion of people in its predominant sense within the Left Front in fact contributes to preserving the status of noncitizen for blacks, Arabs, and Muslims, that is to say the relegation outside of the political field of a wide margin of the most disadvantaged social classes. An eloquent example: the acerbic comments of the leader of the Left Front with regard to a recent rebellion in the Amiens suburb where populations descended from immigration are particularly present. The grounds for the revolt, unleashed by a routine traffic inspection, was police harassment, of which the inhabitants of working-class neighborhoods are constant victims, especially if they are not white. As is often the case in circumstances like these, a school and some cars were set on fire while sixteen police were wounded in the violent confrontations. Without finding the least justification for the rioters' anger, Jean-Luc Mélanchon characterized them all simply as "cretins," "buffoons," and "servants of capitalism." During a debate that took place at the "Estivales citoyennes 2012 de Front de gauche," Félix Boggio Éwanjé-Épée and Stella Magliani-Belkacem put their finger on the problem: "What is there behind the extremely violent and discrediting terms of Jean-Luc Mélanchon? What is behind these insults is the idea that these youth are not part of the 'people' that his project brings together, that this revolt is not legitimate. That is already to sign up on the wrong side in relationship to the demands expressed by these revolts."[4]

From the point of view of a leftist politics attempting to bring together "those at the bottom," the reference to a homogeneous or potentially homogeneous people is quite obviously a dead end. Whereas for the populations descended from immigration, national assimilation within a single "French people" is not the order of the day, the potency of the national idea, with racial connotations, remains extremely strong within the subordinate classes of "French stock." Refusing to take that into account, as the leftists militants do who think that everything is resolved in the socioeconomic question and that the evil ideologies—of the "communitarians" and national-racists—will evaporate in the dynamic of social struggles, is hardly a responsible position. This process is hobbled by the reasons that lead so many workers and unemployed to vote against their "objective interests," reasons that have so much to do with notions of respect, honor, dignity, and social recognition.

How to Be French Without Being French?

From the point of view of the "colonized within," the strategic difficulty is no less acute. It already arose in segregationist America. To the black integrationist leaders, Malcolm X retorted, "But my old man, how can you consider yourself an American when you have never been treated as an American in this country? . . . Let us suppose that ten men were sitting down, were in the middle of eating dinner, and I came in and went to sit down at their table. They ate; but in front of me there was an empty plate. Is the fact that we are all sitting at the same table enough to make us all diners? I am not dining since no one is letting me take my share of the meal. It isn't enough to be sitting at the same table as those eating dinner to be a diner."[5] That is exactly what the November 2005 rioters were expressing in their own way by conspicuously tearing up their French identity cards in front of the television cameras. Malcolm X had many occasions for repeating this metaphor. We can find it again in the speeches he made as the spokesperson for the Nation of Islam when he defended a separatist perspective, but he would continue to use it even after he had renounced separatism. From then on, he would use the term "Afro-Americans," not without ambiguity, to designate the blacks of the United States, not to signify that henceforth blacks and whites would be part of the same people, the same nation, but on the contrary to mark the difference and assert the need for blacks to have forms of autonomous authority available to them even while participating, with whites, in the same popular sovereignty. Malcolm X died without having resolved the questions that such a process raises.[6]

The same questions arise in France. When one is a racial minority, how does one conceive a politics for oneself in an institutional space shared with the whole population?[7] This strategic question is all the more complicated as it arises differently depending upon whose point of view one adopts, that of the white majority or that of the neo-indigenous. It will find a response shared by all the French population only as the result of a decolonialization process that over a long transition period will involve a dynamic and conflictual compromise between the people and *the peoples* of France, based on a reconstruction of the political community taking into account and institutionalizing the multiple national, cultural, and identitary references.

An alternative leftist politics would not know how to be satisfied with a nonrepressive immigration policy or with taking measures against racial discrimination. All that is imperative of course, as is the necessary rupture with the French state's engagement in imperial politics. But if it wants to be effective, the left must also agree that it will not make the economy another political tool of "national identity." I am deliberately using this term that has been exploited by the Sarkozy right to justify its racist politics. Because in truth, the response that was made to it was very inadequate. Indeed it was not adequate to reveal the aims or to denounce the mystifications. On the contrary, it was necessary to seize the national question for reinterrogation from a decolonial perspective.[8] It was necessary to introduce the plural of the notion of people, to combine, within a revamped definition of popular sovereignty, the redistribution of economic and social powers and the redistribution of cultural and symbolic powers. To assert that in France all cultures now have the right to blossom hardly makes sense if, following the example of the dominant "French culture," those other cultures do not "penetrate" the state, if legal forms of "self-determination" do not emerge as well, ensuring minorities the necessary authority to develop their cultures and their visions of the world. The principle of collective cultural rights, partially recognized today for regional minorities, could be recognized as well for the minorities without territory. To claim, moreover, that in France all denominations have the same rights is a hoax that it is urgent for the left to denounce, not to "radicalize" secularism but to finally consider religious beliefs as legitimate social needs.

Another large question is surely that of "French history" and of its nationalizing and racializing function. It is not a matter of granting the history of minorities a small place in school textbooks, or of "reconciling memories" (how can the memory of the colonists be reconciled with the memory of the colonized?), or even less of abandoning history to the historians, that is to say, removing it from politics. But rather of returning to the multiple histories of the French populations their entire place in the state and in society.

These are only a few courses of action that need to be deepened, widened, and clarified in such a way as to conceive of what, in the area of "identity," could be stated in terms of dynamic compromise, capable of opening the horizons for decolonization.

For the left, the issue is not one of reforming itself, or of being more radical within a matrix that finally remains unchanged, but of engaging in a true cultural revolution from within. I do not doubt the generosity of some of its elements, but in politics generosity is never very far from paternalism or paternalism from domination. Thus it will be necessary for it to break with the illusion of its own universality, as it will be necessary for it to learn that it is not the expression of a single oppressed people but an expression, among other things, of white privilege that it must learn to fight if it aspires to making a political alliance conceivable between the white working classes and the working classes descended from immigration, around a project capable of establishing the actual sovereignty of a people both one and multiple.

6

THE POPULISM THAT IS

NOT TO BE FOUND

JACQUES RANCIÈRE

A day does not go by when one does not hear denounced in Europe the risk of populism. For all that, it is not easy to grasp exactly what this word means. In Latin America in the 1930s and 1940s it served to designate a certain mode of government, establishing between a people and its leader a relationship of direct embodiment, passing over and above the forms of parliamentary representation. This mode of government for which Vargas of Brazil and Perón of Argentina were the archetypes was rechristened "twenty-first-century socialism" by Hugo Chávez. But what in Europe today falls under the name of populism is something else. It is not a mode of government. On the contrary, it is a certain attitude of rejection in relationship to prevailing governmental practices. What is a populist, as defined today by our governmental elites and their ideologues? Through all the word's vacillations, the dominant discourse seems to characterize it by three essential traits: a style of speaking that addresses itself directly to the people, going beyond its representatives and notables; the assertion that governments and ruling elites are more concerned with their own interests than the state; an identitary rhetoric that expresses fear and rejection of foreigners.

It is clear nevertheless that these three traits are not necessarily linked. An entity called the people exists that is the source of power and the recognized interlocutor in political discourse: that is what our constitutions assert, and it is the conviction that republican and socialist orators of the past deployed without reservation. It is tied to no form of racist sentiment or xenophobia whatsoever. Our politicians think more about their own careers than the future of their citizens, and our governments live in symbiosis with the representatives of large financial interests: it takes no demagogue to proclaim that. The same newspapers that denounce "populist" leanings provide us with the most detailed evidence of it day after day. On their side, the heads of the government and the state sometimes accused of populism, like Berlusconi or Sarkozy, are very careful not to spread the "populist" idea that the elite are corrupt. The term "populism" does not serve to characterize a defined political force. On the contrary, it benefits from the amalgams that it allows between political forces that range from the extreme right to the radical left. It does not designate an ideology or even a coherent political style. It serves simply to draw the image of a certain people.

Because "the people" does not exist. What exist are diverse or even antagonistic figures of the people, figures constructed by privileging certain modes of assembling, certain distinctive traits, certain capacities or incapacities: an ethnic people defined by the community of land or blood; a vigilant herding people by good pastureland; a democratic people putting to use the skills of those who have no particular skills; an ignorant people that the oligarchs keep at a distance; and so on. The notion of populism itself constructs a people characterized by the formidable alloy of a capacity—the brute force of great number—and an incapacity—the ignorance attributed to that same great number. The third trait, racism, is essential for this construction. It is a matter of showing the democrats, always suspected of having their heads in the clouds, what is in truth the broad mass of people: a pack possessed by a primary drive of rejection that is aimed simultaneously at the rulers whom it declares traitors, lacking an understanding of the complexity of political mechanisms, and at the foreigners whom it fears through an atavistic attachment to a way of life threatened by demographic, economic, and social change. The notion of populism effects at the least cost this synthesis between a people hostile to those governing and a people enemy to "others" in general. To do so it must again present an image of the people developed at the end of the nineteenth century by thinkers like Hippolyte Taine and Gustave Le Bon, frightened by the Commune of Paris and the rise of the workers' movement: the one of ignorant masses impressed by the resonant words of the "agitators" and led to extreme violence by the circulation of uncontrolled rumors and contagious fears.

These epidemic outbreaks by the blind masses led by charismatic leaders were clearly very far from the reality of the workers' movement that they aimed at stigmatizing. But they are not any more appropriate for describing the reality of racism in our societies. Whatever the grievances expressed daily regarding those called immigrants, and especially the "suburban youth," they are not expressed in popular mass demonstrations. What earns the name of racism today in our country is essentially the conjunction of two things. First of all there are the forms of discrimination in employment and housing that are practiced perfectly in sterile offices, away from any mass pressure. Then there is a whole panoply of state measures: restricted entry to the country; refusal to give papers to those who have worked, participated, and paid taxes in France for years; restrictions on the right of birthplace; double penalty; laws against the foulard and burqa; imposed numbers of border escorts; breaking up nomadic camps. Some good souls on the left like to see these measures as an unfortunate concession made by those in power to the extreme "populist" right for "electioneering" reasons. But none of them were taken under pressure from mass movements. They are part of a strategy belonging to the state, belonging to the balance that our states go to great lengths to maintain between free circulation of capital and constraints on the free circulation of populations. Their essential goal is indeed to jeopardize a part of the population with regard to its rights to work and to citizenship, to put together a population of workers who can always be sent back home and of French who have no guarantee of remaining French.

These measures are supported by an ideological campaign, justifying this reduction of rights by the evidence of nonadherence to the traits characterizing national identity. But it is not the "populists" of the National Front that unleashed this campaign. It is the intellectuals of the so-called left who came up with the infallible argument: those people are not truly French since they are not secular. The secularism that not so long ago defined the state's rules of conduct has thus become a quality that individuals possess, or that they lack by reason of their belonging to a community. Marine Le Pen's recent "slip" regarding those Muslims at prayer occupying our streets like the Germans between 1940 and 1944 is instructive in this respect. It really only condenses into a concrete image a discursive sequence (Muslim = Islamist = Nazi) that is present almost everywhere in so-called republican prose. The so-called populist extreme right does not express a specific xenophobic passion emanating from the depths of the body popular; it is a satellite that profits from the strategies of the state and the distinguished intellectual campaigns. Our states base their legitimacy today on their ability to ensure security. But this legitimization has as its correlate the obligation to show at every moment the monster that threatens us, to maintain the continual feeling of an insecurity that mixes the risks of economic crisis and unemployment with those of black ice and formamide so that it can all culminate in the supreme threat of the Islamist terrorist. The extreme right only has to fill in the colors of skin and blood on the standard portrait drawn by governmental measures and ideological prose.

That is why neither the "populists" nor the people represented by the ritual denunciations of populism truly correspond to their definition. But that hardly matters to those who raise its specter. Beyond the polemics on immigrants, communitarianism, or Islam, their essential goal is to merge the very idea of a democratic people with the image of the dangerous masses. It is to draw the conclusion that we must leave matters up to those who govern us and that any contestation of their legitimacy and their integrity is the open door to totalitarianism. "Better a banana republic than a fascist France" was one of the most grim anti-Le Pen slogans of April 2002. The current campaign on the mortal dangers of populism aims to justify in theory the idea that we have no other choice.

CONCLUSION

FRAGILE COLLECTIVITIES,

IMAGINED SOVEREIGNTIES

KEVIN OLSON

Popular politics is based on a set of fragile, changeable associations: forms of mobilization, collective action, public opinion, and symbolic protest. These are framed as different forms of collectivity—peoples, nations, publics, crowds, masses, mobs—which inhabit our collective imagination in different ways. They differ in their durability and rectitude: the composition of various groups, the ways they act, their forms of association, the normative nuances of our attitudes toward them. Among these, the people is one with a storied and privileged history.

I would like to raise an issue that haunts many discussions of this subject without making its presence fully felt. Others have managed to talk around what is in many ways the key issue: the meaning and significance of the people. The reason we ask "What is a people?," the reason we attach significance and meaning to this particular abstraction, is precisely because of its normative character. We think of peoples as having powers, and we accord them a significance not shared by other collectivities. Collectivities like "the people" are surrounded by a complex aura of meaning. Clearly, if the answer to the question "What is a people?" comes back *only* in the form of a discussion about universality, incompleteness, the partitioning of society, class and group fractions, and various other questions about group composition, then the most important point is being missed. That is the answer registered in terms of the meaning and normative force of the people. To address that question we must attempt to capture something ineffable about our own thoughts and practices, something that is both persistent and fleeting. These are the political imaginaries that create "the people" and give it normative force.

To tease this important theme out of the discussion that has come before, (1) I begin by examining the rather different concerns of Alain Badiou and Pierre Bourdieu, both of whom focus on the composition and fragility of the people. (2) Judith Butler and Georges Didi-Huberman move us beyond this focus on the composition of collectivities, bringing important insights about performativity and sensibility to our understanding of the people. (3) These insights set the stage for my own concerns about the normative character of the people, the senses in which it is imagined as having important forms of power. Viewed from this perspective, the people can be thought of as a kind of "imagined sovereignty," one that combines ideas of collectivity and normative force. Only by tracing the development of these ideas in our collective imagination do we understand why the people occupies such a special place in our political tradition.

Fragile Collectivities: Fractions, Distinctions, and Parts with No Part

"The people" is a plastic and flexible notion that can be deployed in many different ways. This is well documented in Alain Badiou's "Twenty-Four Notes on the Uses of the Word 'People.'" He explores the grammar of this term's use, which allows it to be bent in a number of directions. When this takes a nationalist form, it falls under suspicion. Locutions like "the French people" or "the Russian people" merely document the inertia of a past political movement ossified in a state, according to Badiou. This "national adjective + people" refers back to a historical past of actual political energies that were dissipated in state formation. The term is now deployed without actual referent to legitimate this state so that it may serve the needs of capital. "The people" is deeply bound up with the state in this sense, causing Badiou to give it the name "official people." By virtue of its depoliticization and orientation toward consumption, Badiou dubs this the middle class. Thus in note 19 we find, "The middle class is the 'people' of the capitalist oligarchies."[1] These are the "false people," Badiou says, because of their passive and diffuse nonexistence as a political force and their function in legitimating a system that is, by implication, illegitimate.

A host of other categories stand in contrast. "The people's people" are the excluded and invisible; more specifically, they are invisible from the perspective of the official people. There are also people who mobilize against colonization or empire, guided by a vision of a national people. This is a different deployment of "national adjective + people."[2]

Universalism hovers on the edge of Badiou's discussion. A fraction of the people mobilizes itself and overcomes the passivity of state cooptation by declaring itself "the people." This is a people defined by "the future perfect of a nonexistent state," in the case of an anticolonial struggle aiming at national liberation, or "abolishing the existing state," in the case of a group excluded from the "official" people, one that Badiou claims would aim at communist politics.[3]

Badiou maintains an awareness of the way modes of distinction shape this concept. Here his work intersects with that of Pierre Bourdieu. Bourdieu is also interested in language in use. He parses out the social dynamics underlying such usages, focusing on "popular" rather than "the people." The shift from noun to adjective is important. The grammar of "the people" is a constitutive grammar:

it constitutes groups by naming them. "Popular," in contrast, is a weapon in the ongoing struggles of already-existing groups. It traces the social dynamics through which groups are valued and revalued in social space.[4] Thus when we encounter difficulties in the use of "popular," its politics are already apparent. Those politics concern the "proper" use of the adjective, where "proper" itself is a nexus of dispute and is patterned by the very mechanisms of power and distinction that create groups. "Popular," then, is an object of struggle with constitutive significance.

The deployment of "popular" that most occupies Bourdieu's attention is to classify forms of language use. Here popular is defined relationally as that which is excluded from "legitimate" language, which is to say, language formed according to the "accepted" or "proper" rules. It is also generated as an active strategy of defiance, a refusal to interpolate oneself into the social order structured by legitimate language. This is the choice to be a skilled speaker of a devalued idiom rather than a poor speaker of an officially sanctioned one. In these senses, language is both a marker of social difference and a principal stake in struggles over it.

The people never becomes a political subject for Bourdieu. It remains within the ambit of an ascribed category of social identity, chiefly a devalued one. In this, he revitalizes a much older view, one that had great currency in the France of the late ancien régime. Eighteenth-century ironists like Voltaire and Gabriel-François Coyer characterized the people as an abandoned, stigmatized class fraction. Coyer's 1755 *Dissertation sur la nature du peuple*, for instance, shows a well-tuned sensitivity to the mechanisms of group distinction. Various occupational groups except themselves from "the people," leaving farmers, domestics, and artisans. Even among the artisans, those who make luxury goods for the rich claim a refinement that excepts them from the people. Left behind is "the mass of the people."[5] These are the ones, as Voltaire put it a decade later, "who have only their arms for sustenance."[6]

Coyer's commentary is post-Marxist ahead of its time, tracing out social distinction as a matter of group formation rather than class. Like Bourdieu, Coyer understands these dynamics as moves in a game of better-than and worse-than. They are attempts to consolidate group identities while simultaneously revaluing them. Coyer's greatest sensitivity is to the cultural politics of social classification. Such was society at the end of the Bourbon monarchy; such is society under global neoliberalism for Bourdieu. *Plus ça change...*

The similarities and contrasts between these trenchant social critics is an interesting one. Bourdieu recapitulates, with considerably greater theoretical sophistication, insights from several centuries past. (Here his position as a successor of Marx is a decided advantage.) From this perspective, it is interesting to speculate about the parallels between the ancien régime and our own: history recounts a time when resentment at social distinction and dispossession explodes in an orgy of political change, tearing down a decadent regime of aristocratic privilege at the hands of the people. But that is a different topic. For the moment, it is sufficient to note the form of political analysis we get from this view, found in both its eighteenth-and twenty-first-century variants. That is a pointed critique of the politics of marginalization and deprivation. It delineates the ways ("social") distinction is a mechanism of ("political") depoliticization and exclusion. The social is the political and vice versa. For Coyer, this results in an attitude toward the people that, he ironically implies, leaves us wondering whether they are rational at all or simply animals.[7] For Bourdieu, it shows up in a kind of voluntary self-silencing, in which people conclude they are unqualified to participate in politics or even to have political opinions.[8] His analysis is particularly trenchant because he shows how particular group identities are internalized as forms of conscious self-exclusion from politics. In these cases, being a member of the people is the opposite of being politically engaged.

It is equally important to note what we do not get here, something that is more present for Badiou: attention to the ways collectivities function as political agents. There is no account of how "the people" becomes . . . a people. Or, more rigorously, the people for Bourdieu remains a self-marginalized, devalued social remainder, not a political agent. Bourdieu would likely argue that this is not a theoretical overstatement so much as a frank assessment of the ways material dispossession takes on social, cultural, psychic, and political form. Yet that answer is not good enough, because occasionally the people do form a people; occasionally the marginalized and scattered remainder becomes a unified, self-aware political force; and we leave too much on the table to ignore such occurrences and blind ourselves to this other important sense of the people.

Of course, the phenomenon of collective political action is not well developed by Badiou either. He traces the attribution of peoplehood through a number of political uses, delineating its problematic and progressive deployments. The paradigms he posits are rather stylized, however: the state serves capital and is thus legitimated by a passive mass. These paradigms nonetheless serve to draw important lines between passive and active collectivities, which Badiou reads as the distinction between (passive) legitimation and (active) mobilization. Here the advantages of his approach are sold short by the uses he makes of it: a grammatical analysis of the deployment of "the people"-as-language is pressed into the service of a relatively heavy-handed political analysis (though one not without merits). What Badiou best captures is the mobile, malleable character of "the people" as an element of language. He focuses thereby on the senses in which the people can be symbolically represented and pressed into various uses.

Two Moments of the People: Performativity and the Imaginary

Judith Butler's thinking about the people traces a different arc. Rather than examining the composition of peoples, she focuses on the acts and processes through which they are created. Performativity occupies center stage here as the means by which peoples posit themselves.

Like Bourdieu and Badiou, Butler notes the constitutive effects of language in the formation of groups. "We, the people," for instance, is an utterance with constitutive effects in the creation of a group. Butler shows that language is not primary in such instances, however. She notes that this kind of expression is not simply a speech act but one preceded by action: "the assembly of bodies, their gestures and movements, their vocalizations, and their ways of acting in concert."[9] It is a performative political enactment that is prior to the speech act itself. This is a politics of bodies assembled in groups, one that amounts to an act of collective self-constitution. It creates an "'anarchist' energy or a permanent principle of revolution within democratic orders," a force that legitimates political representation but always exceeds it.[10] The performance of collectivity also creates the basis for a more familiar and easily identifiable act of self-designation: "we, the people." Collective political action thus precedes the speech act itself: a material performative goes hand in hand with a discursive one. In this sense, Butler's notion of performativity is simultaneously discursive and material. It does not reduce one to the other but emphasizes their distinct and interlocking character.

The complex, discursive-material character of the people is an important insight on Butler's part. She corrects our distorting tendency to see all politics through the lens of the linguistic turn, criticizing the focus on claims and speech acts at the expense of bodies and the politics of the street. The potent political force of people assembled in the square, before the parliament house, in silent vigil, in tent cities, in celebration, protest, or mourning—all of this goes to the core of contemporary politics, and Butler does us the great service of thematizing it as vital to our understanding of the people.

Yet Butler may overstate the importance of materiality in relation to discourse. The discursive constitution of a people—"we [are] the people"—is not necessarily preceded by its performative enactment.

To claim otherwise overestimates the role of embodiment in relation to discourse, according one priority over the other. One phenomenon that is well captured by the linguistic turn, by thinkers as different from one another as Ernesto Laclau and Jürgen Habermas, is the *virtualization* of the people in contemporary politics.[11] There is a tendency for politics to be sublimated into discourse through forms of dispersed and abstract media. We might call this "the work of politics in the age of its technical mediation." This is not to say that thinkers like Laclau and Habermas have the full picture. They overstate the case in the opposite direction, dissolving materiality and practice into abstract forms of discourse, and are much in need of Butler's corrective. But neither should we follow Butler in thinking that physical, corporal enactment must precede discursive self-constitution. The people need not assemble before declaring themselves a people. Rather, we might think of performativity as including material and discursive elements of various kinds. The people is *performed*, but that performance can take many forms: the outdoor politics of the people in the square or the virtualized politics of public opinion formation in electronic media, for example. These forms are mixed and combined in complicated ways—always performed, but in a complex mélange of materiality and discourse.

As rich as Butler's insights about performativity are, they do not go far enough to explain how a people becomes a people. Not present in this insightful analysis are our reasons for saying that an assembled group should have any particular significance. Why should a given group be interpreted as "the people" and accorded a special normative status? Why should we attribute particular force to the claims of such a group? How do we distinguish the performative enactment of the people from any other kind of assembly? Performativity is not enough to account for this in itself, nor is discursive self-assertion.

Earlier generations of political thinkers would have said, "We hold the people to be special and significant because they are sovereign." They would agree with Butler about the anarchist energy and

permanent revolution of the people, attributing it to a form of collective self-direction that was held to be natural or self-evident. This
response is not satisfactory either, of course. It merely begs the question, pushing the burden back another step. It does not explain why
we think that some particular group is the people, or why we think
that this people is sovereign.

Butler would not try to salvage this way of approaching the problem. She has strong objections to the idea of sovereignty, even though
her ideas about anarchist energy and permanent revolution invoke
similar associations. In the company of thinkers like Walter Benjamin, Jacques Derrida, Michel Foucault, and Carl Schmitt, she characterizes sovereignty as a form of absolute mastery and control.[12]
Writing about performativity in language, for instance, she takes
pains to undermine what she has called "sovereign performatives."
They are forms of "absolute and efficacious agency" in language, in
her view. To invoke them, Butler says, is to draw on a fantasy about a
return of sovereign power, a power that in language has always been
a fantasy.[13] This fantasy invokes a conceptual frame that was rightly
rejected by Michel Foucault, she says, because it is built on a notion
of subjectivity that emphasizes the centrality of subjective agency
at the expense of diffuse relations of domination and control. Thus
she draws a sharp line between an absolutist conception of sovereignty and the more ineffable and diffuse power of the people that
she describes.

Butler's objections to this notion of subjectivity lie in an insightful analysis of the sense in which speech acts are insufficient to assert
peoplehood. A speech act is not a self-contained act. The conditions
for their assertion and acceptance are not given in the moment; "the
temporal conditions for making the speech act precede and exceed
the momentary occasion of its enunciation."[14] In other discussions
of performativity and language, she emphasizes the role of convention as that which stands outside of and beyond sovereign subjectivity. The performative force of an utterance is generated from the

conventions that it draws on. No one (singly, individually) exercises sovereignty through speech. Because of the role of convention in creating, stabilizing, and reproducing language, it is not possible purely to exercise one's own will in saying something. That utterance depends upon a reservoir of convention for its meaning and force.

What then about performatives involving "the people"? Are those also modeled on sovereign performativity? Here, Butler deemphasizes language to bring materiality more fully to the fore. In this account, the performativity of the people is not linguistic and conventional but performed through assembly. This does not seem quite right, however. We should not be so quick to reject sovereignty as an analytic concept, nor should we lose sight of convention as a vital part of sovereign performatives. Political sovereignty is built on a long history of convention that has great currency in our culture. To object to the intertwinement between subjectivity and sovereignty is to be distracted by intellectual constructs. The actually-existing commitments of our culture contain many elements that, on closer scrutiny, fit together poorly or do not make sense. A strong conception of subjectivity associated with notions of absolute sovereign control is surely one of those problematic ideas. However it is important to remember that there is much more in operation in our shared imagination of politics than these (purified, rationally reconstructed) ideals.

Absolutist conceptions of sovereignty have always been counterfactual assertions, more attempts to save some waning system of authority than descriptions of reality. Thus, Hobbes and Filmer, for instance, articulated powerful defenses of absolute monarchy as a rearguard action against a seventeenth-century democratic revolution. To dismiss sovereignty based on such narrow and counterfactual conceptions is unfortunate. It singles out a small group of (historically embattled) conceptions among many, only to dismiss them, leaving aside the scattered plethora of other forms that proliferated after the age of kings. Today, sovereignty is one of the principal ways we understand ideas like "the people," which is not to say in any absolute or unitary form. Rather it gives us a historically situated vocabulary for examining the genealogy of such ideas. It is precisely this history that traces the conventions around the people. If we are serious about bringing forward Butler's admirable insights about the people and performativity, we must view sovereignty (in piecemeal, malleable, nonabsolutist form) as a principal locus of such convention. We must take a broader view of the noise and fiber of actually-existing cultural contents, including the ways that sovereignties permeate our understanding of what it means to act as and declare ourselves to be the people.

For help in this endeavor, let us turn to a second moment of the people. Georges Didi-Huberman thematizes the ways the people can be "rendered sensible," which is to say brought to the focus of our attention. For him, this is not necessarily a matter of making present, in the sense of bringing into visibility something that is fully there but obscure. Rather it is a critical and problematizing sensibility. This can be a matter of what he refers to, following Walter Benjamin, as a dialectic of images, one that loosens our grasp on received opinion by problematizing the sensible.[15] It can also consist in opening up alternative perceptions of history, critically interrogating the representation of the people. Michel de Certeau, Michel Foucault, and Arlette Farge are put forward by Didi-Huberman as exemplary of this problematizing practice. Rendering something sensible can involve bringing to attention things lacked and desired. In the case of the people, for instance, he follows Maurice Blanchot in noting that the powerlessness of the people itself can be rendered sensible. Similarly, for Didi-Huberman rendering sensible can involve bringing to our senses something that does not make sense. In these cases, Didi-Huberman characterizes rendering sensible as a twofold movement: being moved emotionally and moved to thought.[16] There is, in other words, a motivational-critical force to rendering sensible, one that challenges existing truths and images while rendering these problematizations vivid to us.

Didi-Huberman's ethos of problematization holds particularly for representative abstractions like "the people." He is careful to specify that the people does not exist "as a unity, identity, totality, or generality"; it is a nonidentity that is always incomplete.[17] Otherwise put, the people should not be subsumed into the unity of one concept. He sides with thinkers like Bataille, Blanchot, and Nancy, who problematize notions of collectivity that are conceptualized as simple communion or substantial unity.[18]

Didi-Huberman's focus thus falls on peoples in the plural, by which he means specific and unique peoples. His attention is directed to marginalized and invisible peoples, those without name, without papers, without lodging, without rights, and without images. He often refers to this in Jacques Rancière's idiom of "the part with no part." His project of rendering the people sensible, he says, is to return such peoples to the rank of full status as political subjects. In this sense, his concerns intersect with those of Badiou, Bourdieu, Coyer, and Rancière. Interestingly he does not characterize this project as focusing on equality but on what he calls the upwelling of heterogeneity (*surgissement de l'hétérogène*).[19] The point is not to render equal but to bring to the fore the wide variety of what is marginalized and hidden from sensibility.

Didi-Huberman is careful not to hypostatize representation. His reference to rendering sensible should be read as a careful choice: not simply visibility but a broader form of sensibility that includes aspects of attention, classification, and prioritization. It includes practices that might otherwise be classified as cognition or perception, and it frames sensibility as an inherently intersubjective practice. It is no mistake, in this light, that Didi-Huberman refers at various points to the *imaginary* character of peoples. He references the differentiated, social character of this idea in Cornelius Castoriadis's work.[20] Castoriadis talks about the imaginary without reducing it to a logic of identities or a positivist myth of representational transparence. He renders the imaginary social, a space of community in which community itself is always under negotiation. By associating his project with the imaginary, on one hand, and community, on the other, Didi-Huberman makes clear how rendering sensible relates to peoples. First, he is interested in the broadest register of the sensible world we share in common. Second, he frames a notion of community in which imaginary classifications are always in play, both potentially hypostatizing *and* always open to critique. And third, he is keenly aware of the way these two things come together to render certain groups ("peoples") marginal, of lesser value, or invisible. Thus the political logic of rendering sensible has a strong, critical focus on forms of social exclusion, picking up themes shared with others but revealing their deployment and reproduction in the imaginary domain.

In this sense, Didi-Huberman's critical focus on representations in the broadest sense provides a corrective to a narrower emphasis on language in the constitution of peoples. The world-constituting power of language carries over to political collectivities, particularly in the form of naming. This is reflected in the perspectives of Butler and Badiou. Bourdieu displays it in a different way: social identity is quietly duplexed onto language use, not in the form of naming but in the minute variations of usage that code social identity. This is a very incomplete picture, however. Without rejecting language, Didi-Huberman pushes outside its bounds to reveal the symbolic elements at work in the formation of political collectivities.

Didi-Huberman's emphasis on forms of representation does impose certain limits on his views, however. One of those is a tendency to view peoples as objects of representation rather than as subjects of politics. They are variously represented, hypostatized, rendered sensible, and/or occluded from sensibility: *objects* of representations. What Didi-Huberman thematizes much less (with some exceptions)[21] is the active, self-constituting dimensions of peoples— the dimensions that capture Butler's attention. This is likely a matter of his framing of the task rather than any deeper narrowness of his views: the idea of rendering sensible is implicitly structured around the accessibility of objects of representation. It is an objectifying perspective, one that comes to seem limited when the objects are peoples.

What is arguably missing from Didi-Huberman's reflections is a particular sense of the people that takes it as a political collectivity with a special normative status. This problem manifests itself in a second limitation of this perspective. Didi-Huberman asserts that there is no "people," only peoples. This is, in certain ways, an important insight about the logic of collective identity and the dangers of fixity and closure. Yet in seeking to prevent us from hypostatizing the people, Didi-Huberman goes too far in the other direction. "The people" has a vital reality in contemporary cultures and constitutes an important part of our modern political imaginaries. To rule that out-of-bounds is to fail to interrogate it as a rich source of meaning in contemporary democratic societies. It is to impose a kind of conceptual correctness where it may not be warranted. Better would be to let the archive speak for itself, noting occasions when "the people" is an organizing concept and others in which "peoples" is more appropriate.

The importance of using both of these concepts in an interpretively astute way is elegantly illustrated by the title of this book. The question posed is not "What are peoples?" but "What is a people?" The choice is an important one, since questions about "peoples" tend to sound like episodes from the philosophical anthropology of the eighteenth and nineteenth centuries: the peoples of the earth, the natural characteristics that separate one people from another, and so forth. The guiding impulse of that project was to catalog different human types. In contrast, investigating the meaning of "a people" is at once vital for interpreting our received common sense and an opportunity to problematize it. Implicit in this undertaking is the idea that there is often some particular people, "the people," that is taken as having singular importance within a given context. This is the idea that guides Jacques Rancière, for instance, when he distinguishes between "the very idea of a democratic people" and political attempts to subvert that idea by merging it with "the image of the dangerous masses."[22] Rancière agrees with Didi-Huberman that there is no "people" as such, yet he is also keenly aware that images of the people circulate in our collective imagination, and some of them exert a powerful normative force in politics. He has traced some of these images in his own work, particularly the diverse essays published in *Les Révoltes Logiques* between 1975 and 1985.[23] Following the consequences of this line of thought, we can say that the people is an imaginary entity; it has a tangible reality for us because we imagine it as such. Investigating the sources of its special, normative character is to inquire into the intersubjective, shared, imaginary construction of the people.

When we ask "What is a people?" we are not asking a purely socio-ontological question: about its formation in the social space of our collective imagination. The social ontology of the people pivots around a crucial, constitutive semantic element. What the people is depends upon what the people *means*. Put otherwise, the most crucial element is the way the people takes on shades of meaning in the ongoing process of construction. To ask questions about the place of the people in our shared imaginaries is thus to ask about the way we construct visions of the people and endow them with meaning. In this sense, the people goes beyond being a simple collective identity that assembles individuals into groups. It is a *meaningful* collectivity that we endow with normative value. The people is important in politics because it has these normative valences, ones that change with time and context, and are thus all the more interesting.

Following Didi-Huberman's inspiration, we should ask about the diffuse and ineffable image of the people that we do share: one that is part of our shared imaginary, our very conception of what politics is and how it functions. That is the question we could see being posed, for instance, by Judith Butler's evocation of the force of the people assembled. We think of such assemblies in some way as "the people." The question is how and why?

In this vein, one can imagine a different kind of rendering sensible of the people. It is something that groups do for themselves, a self-reflexive practice that we might call a *performative* rendering sensible. Such an idea expands Didi-Huberman's insights in Butler's direction. Here we can point out that political demonstrations and other material, public manifestations of the people render sensible and problematize at the same time. They bring forth identities and claims into the public, giving the lie to silences and omissions of public attention. At the same time, the meaning of an assembly or public display is not entirely clear. It has a nonverbal facticity that invites interpretation, just like an image or object. As such, assemblies constitute a form of problematization. They provoke and enter into the public construction of meaning rather than unilaterally providing it. In all of these ways, a Butlerian perspective on performativity can be joined with Didi-Huberman's insights on interpretation and problematization. It turns our attention toward issues of political imaginaries and self-constitution, and especially what happens when the two come together. Didi-Huberman's notion of rendering sensible can be retasked in a project of critique connected to our shared political imaginaries and the ways that they constitute the normative bases for popular politics.

Imagined Sovereignties

A great deal of attention has been devoted to the fragile, fleeting nature of the people as a collectivity. It is clear, however, that the instabilities of the people are not simply a problem of composition. They are not a problem of collectivity as such: of its unstable and shifting makeup, of the tendency of the affluent to except themselves from the whole, leaving only those who have no part. As we have seen in Didi-Huberman's work, the people is very much grounded in the way we perceive and value particular kinds of collectivities. This work insightfully thematizes the representational, imaginary, and symbolic aspects of the people. To elaborate the project I have been pointing toward so far, I would like to push Didi-Huberman's insights further in this direction, approaching the people as a more general normative category.

We need to account for the ways that the people takes on normative colorations—the ways it becomes a politically significant collectivity. This is tantamount to asking how we understand the difference between a mere gathering of individuals—say, a bowling league or a sales convention—and "the people" in its fully sanctified sense. In Badiou's language, we are trying to discern what changes when a minority detachment declares itself the people. From Butler's perspective, we are trying to determine what makes an assembly into the people. In both cases, we are asking how a group adopts the normative mantle of the people, claiming authorization to act in the name of a collectivity with a special normative status. We are trying to determine what act of transubstantiation creates these normatively special collectivities, where otherwise we would see only individuals assembled.

To understand this phenomenon, we need to examine the normative background that endows the people with its special status. There is a host of historically specific terms that describe aspects of this: popular sovereignty, "the power of the people," constituent power, the subtle normative shadings of related terms like nations, publics, crowds, masses, and mobs. For shorthand, we might call these *sovereign imaginaries*. They include the absolutist conceptions of sovereignty criticized by Butler, as well as various fragmentary, piecemeal, part-wise authorizations that are ineffable because they are nowhere explicitly granted. Such ideas are part of the reservoir of our background assumptions about political action: imaginaries about who is entitled to act and on what basis.

At the center of this heterogeneous ensemble we find "the people," with all of the subtleties and instabilities of composition that we have already examined. Also revealed here are the constructions that surround the people and invest it with normative powers: "the power of the people," the sanctity of foundings and new beginnings, as well as other forms of rectitude and authorization. These powers accrete through slow processes of formation that lead us to think of the people as a distinctive collectivity and an important political actor.

To see how sovereign imaginaries develop over time, we must examine them in their historical specificity. The notion of the people takes on a politically significant role in modern Europe in the late middle ages, when it functions to acclaim the king. With the gradual disintegration of monarchy in the seventeenth and eighteenth centuries, the people first constitutes a euphemized criticism of royal rule, then its competitor, and finally its replacement. These themes transform in new ways in the early nineteenth century. In some cases they furnish a basis for the progressive breakup of colonialism and the host of new sovereignties that it spawned. In other ways, nineteenth-century nationalism pushes the people aside in favor of the nation as a collectivity of choice. At the same time, subnational collectivities like crowds and masses become increasingly prominent, largely as objects of fear in the barricade politics of revolutionary Europe and the anxious imaginations of early social scientists.[24]

These imagined normativities enter a broad field of action as they arrive in the twentieth century. There is the mobilization of the people in the Russian Revolution and the subsequent formation of Soviets that was celebrated by Hannah Arendt.[25] More perversely, there is the popular basis of National Socialism in Germany and the widespread popular acclaim of fascism in Italy. There are popular insurgencies in Hungary in 1956 and Czechoslovakia in 1968, then again across the whole Soviet empire in 1989. The unworking of colonialism across the globe in the nineteenth and twentieth centuries furnishes a whole different set of paradigms for imagining the people and its powers. More recently, we have Tahrir Square and the rest of the Arab Spring, pro-democracy protests in Hong Kong, and anti-austerity demonstrations in Europe. The Internet and other communication technologies have created wikis, blogs, and other postindustrial knowledge projects of all kinds, in which the people stands for new forms of decentralized, democratized epistemology. In all of these instances, the people and its powers are imagined in new and different ways.

This historical kaleidoscope reveals important aspects of the ways that political collectivities are imagined. It includes not only notions of collectivity itself—say, "peoples"—but also the normative statuses with which they are endowed—their "powers." Most prominently, we see that the power of the people is an unstable set of historically contingent, changing cultural and material constructions that are continually problematized even while they are being elaborated. They are formed out of a complex web of symbolic contents, acts, and practices of imagination. Such efforts of imagination are always partial, incomplete, more a form of symbolic and material politics than a fully worked out, coherent doctrine.

Consider, for instance, a pivotal moment in this history: the formation of modern ideas of the people in eighteenth-century France. Under the ancien régime, "the people" is a term of art in a genre of political criticism. It used by public intellectuals like Voltaire and Coyer to attack the monarchy in a backhanded way, euphemizing politics as a form of social critique and removing its sting with humor and irony. These writings are very much a part of the intellectual scene of salons and *sociétés de pensée*. As conditions change, however, the monarchy weakens and the people is pressed into a different function. It now becomes a conceptual means to retheorize sovereignty. Gone is the unified agency and will of the king; in its place steps a rather problematic, fraught attempt to universalize the people and endow it with the kind of normative status that the king used to bear. Conceptual pieces and remainders of royal sovereignty are repurposed to create new notions of the people, with somewhat mixed and unstable results.[26]

In this era, the people and its powers are articulated *within* a set of unresolved problematics. These ideas are created to take the place of royal sovereignty; they try to respond to the problematic situation at the same time that they are inscribed within it. As a result, there is continued unsettlement and controversy over the composition of the collective identities. Throughout this time period, there is substantial disagreement about what the people actually means— who it signifies, who is included, on what basis, by what right. This includes often paradoxical attempts to claim its universal character simultaneously with forms of differentiation. In this sense there is a complex web of associations between sovereignty and collective identity. Universalism and particularity compete with one another. There is confusion whether sovereignty and power proceed from "all the people" or various partisan movements, factions, or insurgencies. There are questions whether parts of the people might be disqualified from sovereignty, or by extension, certain material conditions might disqualify specific groups. Such attempts to settle the meaning and composition of the people are also attempts to settle the question of sovereignty.

The doctrines descended from those revolutionary events in eighteenth-century France imagine the people in an implicitly exclusionist way conditioned by a history of colonialism that reaches back before the Revolution. Thus we see the kinds of tensions that Sadri Khiari identifies: constructions of the people that default to an unmarked white European imaginary, requiring marked exceptions for anyone of a different identity. Khiari notes the implicit exclusion of black, Arab, and Muslim French citizens from "the French people" because they do not fit the imagined identity category. This, he says, happens in an almost subliminal way: someone descended from "French stock" can easily identify with the French people by claiming a privileged relation with the nation-state, whereas a Malian-French or Senegalese-French citizen cannot make the same claim without considerable cultural dissonance. To subvert these imaginaries,

Khiari insightfully notes the need for a "redistribution of cultural and symbolic powers" to bring nationality under interrogation from a "decolonial" perspective.[27] His work brings an important historical element, the colonial history of Europe, to contemporary constructions of the people. It thus draws attention to race as a principal way of not having a part in contemporary societies. It is also implicitly focuses attention on the ways that the people is *imagined*: in this case, as durable, national-racial imaginaries that are warped by internal tensions even though they are lived by millions of Europeans.

The value of tracing such transformations is to observe how the power of the people is imagined as a *normative* construction—as having an inherent value, natural rectitude, or obligatory force. The people are imagined as having power, and that power can vary considerably in its forms, sources, and concentrations. Attempts to settle the meaning and composition of the people are also attempts to attach normative connotations to them. Power is created with the people.

We can call the processes of constructing the normative background of sovereignties "normatization."[28] It creates value in the political imaginary by forging connections between collectivities of various kinds and other ideas and practices. These associations and projections can be made with a space or territory; they can be counterfactual or actual; they can be projected into the future or the past, articulated across space, time, and collective identity in characteristic, distinct, and variable ways. Such associations can include different arrangements of national and territorial space, different appeals to temporality, both in a past-oriented nostalgic mode and a future-oriented, prospective one, or association with other normative values. What lies in common to all of these variations is the creation of a collectivity as having a normative character. The form it takes is a variable and characteristic feature of the particular case under consideration.

In this sense, postulating a political identity can itself be a strategy of normatization. It can project that identity into the past to naturalize it and give it value, or project it into the future as a goal worthy of completion, one that has value now, counterfactually, by virtue of the expectation that it will be completed in the future. A whole set of fantasies and imaginations can be called into play in complicated ways: heroic pasts, sanctified founding moments, future ideal states. All of these play on identity within a politics of meaning. In such cases political identity is less the point than are the processes of normatization that invoke it. Demands for identity are a proxy for the discursive and practical negotiation of sovereign imaginaries. These are practices of imagination that articulate new visions of politics. They are a self-referential, self-reinforcing practice that creates the imaginary bases of popular power.

Consider, for example, the creative ways that normatization endows a collectivity with force by invoking time. Locating one's people or nation in an ancient past, for instance, gives it a kind of naturalized value.[29] More radically, such a community can be located in an eternal past, as Emmanuel Sieyès does in his famous essay on the Third Estate.[30] Past-looking temporalities can also reference a more specific point in time, drawing on the special character of a privileged historical starting point, as in stories of revolutionary founding. Employed in a more abstract sense, this is also the central normative device of social contract theory.

Temporality can be used in a future-oriented sense as well. Here the people defines a goal to be completed or a potential to be realized. In this construction, the people is endowed with normativity by virtue of its future promise.[31] Something like this strategy operates implicitly in many criticisms of the fragmented and exclusionary character of present peoples. It highlights forms of distinction and exclusion as a way of pointing toward a world in which they will be overcome.

The people can also be imagined as having a normative status by associating it with concepts of space. This is particularly true when a people alleges itself always to have existed on some territory. It puts into play a double strategy of normatization, in which time is combined with space to naturalize the particular group in a double sense. It taps into some notion, never well articulated, that ancient territorial claims confer a material durability on that people, which in turn creates a presumption of rectitude for its present and future actions. Without trying very hard, one can think of many current political conflicts that play on such ideas. Another way to give the people power is to associate them with a bounded, sovereign territory. This "Westphalian" strategy unifies populace, territory, and jurisdiction in a way that taps into some of our most deeply held normative ideals. It forms the idea of a democratically self-regulating people, one in which the subjects of the law are also its authors. Even though such ideas are deeply entrenched in our current political tradition, there is nothing natural or necessary about them. Like other sovereign imaginaries, they have accreted over a long period of time through processes of normatization.

There are many other ways in which the people can take on normative value, too many to detail here. What is important is the more general point that the people acquires its normative force in concrete and often unexpected ways. The paths of normatization cannot be exhaustively described because they are contingent improvisations within particular circumstances. Such improvisations have a strongly practical and material character. Sovereign imaginaries are articulated, inter alia, through particular understandings of time, space, and collective identity, and through association with various other normative concepts. Normativity, in this view, is not a natural characteristic of certain political forms. Rather, it is constructed of a piece with them. The "power of the people," by extension, is a product of particular ways of imagining politics. The normative force of such ideas is created by summoning particular constellations of elements and constructing durable sovereign imaginaries out of them.

Performativity plays a large role in these processes of collective imagination. Political acts and collectivities take their meaning from such imaginaries, which define who, collectively, counts as a politically significant actor. At the same time, such acts and collectivities contribute to creating our sovereign imaginaries. The people takes its power from performativity in a double sense: by drawing on normative imaginaries and by contributing to their creation. The power of the people has a performative dimension, but it also contributes to the background of shared meanings against which other performances are understood. Put otherwise, it helps to construct the matrix of significations within which practice is perceived. When it comes to collectivity, action can help to constitute the intersubjective, normative basis of reality. It does something in the (intangible, intersubjective) world. Actions of certain sorts exercise a constitutive influence on our political imaginaries.

With these insights, we are back to Butler's idea of the people assembled, but with a different angle of view. One of the most potent effects of collective action, I believe, is to performatively *create* the imaginary bases of popular politics. By acting together, we build a normative basis of ideas about what it *means* to be a people. Chief among these ideas are our images of the significance of collective assembly, popular voice, and the whole range of cases in which we take collective action to have an important and sometimes decisive significance in politics.

This happens in both a compositional and normative sense. It affects what we think "a people" is and what significance we attach to it. Acting like a people can precede and create the imaginary preconditions for being a people. This is similar to the forms of self-authorization described by Jacques Derrida, Jason Frank, and Bonnie Honig.[32] It is not self-authorization in a specific, narrow, legal-political sense, however: not "we hereby create the legal bases for our existence as a people" but rather the long, slow accretion of normative expectations about collectivity and normativity. It is a form of imaginary politics in the broadest, most cultural, and most deeply shared sense.

Having said this, we have not yet erased the problems and tensions that generate ideas of the people. As our ongoing controversies about "the people" indicate, these ideas have never really settled into place. They retain their chafing, problematic form. What it means to be a people, and to act with the authorization of a people, is still problematized and politicized. By exposing this to view, my intention is very much in sympathy with Didi-Huberman's: a kind of rendering sensible of the people and the politics surrounding it. By bringing back to attention the still-problematic nature of the people, we resist attempts to co-opt its special status while reopening questions about the sources and nature of our sovereign imaginaries.

We can now return to the question "What is a people?" A genealogy of popular politics reveals a churning complexity just below the surface of one of our most sacred political ideals. It has a specific history, born out of problematics and remaining so today. The actually-existing imaginaries that populate this history can be quite malleable and contingent. They envision agencies and authorizations in a wide variety of forms. Yet their two crucial elements always travel together: peoples have powers. They are imagined replete with normative force. The people, in short, is an imagined collectivity that bears an imagined sovereignty.

The many different manifestations of the people at the turn of the millennium—the people of the Berlin Wall, Tahrir Square, or Zuccotti Park—all take on significance because of these sovereign imaginaries at the same time that they performatively help to create such imaginaries. The people is a potent creation of our collective imagination, one that is revitalized when it is enacted—and thus reimagined—in new ways.

NOTES

Introduction: This People Which Is Not One

1. E. Laclau, *On Populist Reason* (London: Verso, 2005), 153. For an overview of the frequently untranslatable meanings associated with "people" in different European languages, see the entry "People/Race/Nation," in *Dictionary of Untranslatables: A Philosophical Lexicon*, ed. B. Cassin, trans. J. Lezra, E. Apter, and M. Wood (Princeton: Princeton University Press, 2014), 751–63.

2. J.-J. Rousseau, *On the Social Contract; or, Principles of Political Right*, in *Basic Political Writings*, trans. D. A. Cress (Indianapolis: Hackett, 1987), 147.

3. Ibid., 163. See K. Marx, "On the Jewish Question," in *Early Writings*, trans. R. Livingston and G. Benton (London: Penguin, 1975), 234.

4. Rousseau, *Social Contract*, 148.

5. L. Althusser, "Rousseau: The Social Contract," in *Politics and History*, trans. B. Brewster (London: Verso, 2007), 128–29. Georges Didi-Huberman, who certainly cannot be suspected of Althusserian allegiances, uses the

same term *décalages* (translated as "gaps"), citing the work of Michel de Certeau, to draw attention to the dialectical divisions, fissures, and tears that mark his proposed history of peoples in the plural.

6. Althusser, "Rousseau: The Social Contract," 129. We should add, however, that the many individuals do not exist any more than the oneness of the people prior and externally to the political and ideological processes that constitute the modern category of individuality, which as the holder of inalienable rights would have to be historicized in ways that Althusser is characteristically unwilling to do. Even later, in his definition of ideology as the interpellation of individuals into subjects, Althusser's treatment strangely enough still refuses to insert an element of history into the theory of the subject. See L. Althusser, "Ideology and Ideological State Apparatuses," in *Lenin and Philosophy and Other Essays*, trans. B. Brewster (London: Monthly Review Press, 2001), 127–86.

7. Rousseau, *Social Contract*, 149 (emphasis added).

8. Rousseau, *Émile*, quoted in Althusser, "Rousseau: The Social Contract," 130 (emphasis added).

9. Althusser, "Rousseau: The Social Contract," 132–33.

10. Marx, "On the Jewish Question," in *The Marx–Engels Reader*, ed. R. C. Tucker (New York: Norton, 1978), 46.

11. Althusser, "Rousseau: The Social Contract," 154.

12. Ibid., 155, 159.

13. J. Rancière, *Disagreement: Philosophy and Politics*, trans. J. Rose (Minneapolis: University of Minnesota Press, 1999), 87–88 (translation slightly modified). We can compare Rancière's argument with the way in which another student of Althusser's, Étienne Balibar, mobilizes the antinomy between "man" and "citizen," like the tension between "liberty" and "equality," not as an impasse but as the master key to unlock the politics of what he calls *equaliberty*, in É. Balibar, "'Rights of Man' and 'Rights of the Citizen': The Modern Dialectic of Equality and Freedom," in *Masses, Classes, Ideas: Studies on Politics and Philosophy Before and After Marx*, trans. J. Swenson (New York: Routledge, 1994), 39–59.

14. J. Rancière, "Preface to the English edition," in *Staging the People: The Proletarian and His Double*, trans. D. Fernbach (London: Verso, 2011), 18. In the French original, Rancière uses the expression *les gros mots* ("coarse words") to justify and explain the role of "words today seen as awkward—people, poor, revolution, factory, workers, proletarians—and wielded by outmoded characters." See J. Rancière, "Préface: Les gros mots," in *Les Scènes du peuple (Les Révoltes Logiques, 1975/1985)* (Lyon: Horlieu, 2003), 16. Bourdieu uses the same expression below and adds a further level of sociological reflexivity by studying how the binary distinctions of high and low, delicate and coarse, etc., are very much part and parcel of the linguistic and ideological construction of the "popular," whose "properly political" consequences are always unstable and open to multiple counter-finalities.

15. Rancière, *Disagreement*, 88 (translation modified).

16. L. Althusser, "The 'Piccolo Teatro': Bertolazzi and Brecht. Notes on a Materialist Theatre," in *For Marx*, trans. B. Brewster (London: Verso, 1969), 138n4.

17. E. Laclau, "The Politics of Rhetoric," in *The Rhetorical Foundations of Society* (London: Verso, 2014), 94. Laclau famously generalizes the logic of hegemony as a way of overcoming the class essentialism of orthodox Marxism in his book coauthored with Chantal Mouffe, *Hegemony and Socialist Strategy: Towards a Radical Democratic Politics* (London: Verso, 1985).

18. Rancière, *Disagreement*, 88 (translation modified).

19. Rancière, "Preface to the English Edition," in *Staging the People*, 15.

20. M. Heidegger, *Being and Time: A Translation of* "Sein und Zeit," trans. J. Stambaugh (Albany: State University of New York Press, 1996), 352.

21. M. Heidegger, *Contributions to Philosophy (Of the Event)*, trans. R. Rojcewicz and D. Vallega-Neu (Bloomington: Indiana University Press, 2012), 35. For a chronological interpretation of Heidegger's different uses of the term *Volk* that goes to great lengths to try and separate the philosopher's meditations from the racist biopolitics of Nazism, see H. France-Lanord, "Peuple," in *Le Dictionnaire Martin Heidegger*, ed. P. Arjakovsky, F. Fédier, and H. France-Lanord (Paris: Cerf, 2013), 991–1012.

22. Heidegger, *Contributions to Philosophy*, 42.

23. P. Lacoue-Labarthe, *Heidegger, Art, and Politics: The Fiction of the Political*, trans. C. Turner (Cambridge, Mass.: Basil Blackwell, 1990), 113–14. With the mention of 1967 the author is referring to a talk from this same year that Heidegger delivered in Athens, Greece, entitled "The Provenance of Art and the Destination of Thought," which Lacoue-Labarthe then compares to Heidegger's 1933 "Rectoral Address." In this quote and the next, Lacoue-Labarthe uses "historial" as the translation of the German term *geschichtlich*, which in Heidegger's lexicon refers to the history of Being (*Geschichte*) as opposed to history or historiography in the common sense (*Historie*). At stake is not this or that historical occurrence but the event of being as the ontological possibility of historicity or historiality as such.

24. Ibid., 13 and 112 (translation modified).

25. Ibid., 4–5. See also J.-L. Nancy, *The Inoperative Community*, ed. Peter Connor (Minneapolis: University of Minnesota Press, 1991), and Blanchot's response in *The Unavowable Community*, trans. P. Joris (Barrytown, N.Y.: Station Hill, 1988). Georges Didi-Huberman's idea of "rendering sensible" the absence or powerlessness of the people is openly indebted to this post-Heideggerian line of thinking.

2. You Said "Popular"?

This chapter was originally published in the French as "Vous avez dit 'populaire'?" *Actes de la Recherche en Sciences Sociales* 46 (March 1983): 98–105; reprinted in *Langage et pouvoir symbolique* (Paris: Le Seuil, 2001).

1. The fact that the costs of scientific objectification are particularly elevated for an especially weak—or negative—profit has nothing to do with the state of our knowledge in these matters.

2. *Petit Robert* (1979), xvii.

3. We know the role that similar conscious or unconscious exclusions were able to play in the use that National Socialism made of the word *völkisch*.

4. See H. Bauche, *Le Langage populaire: Grammaire, syntaxe et vocabulaire du français tel qu'on le parle dans le peuple de Paris, avec tous les termes d'argot usuel* (Paris: Payot,

1920); P. Guiraud, *Le Français populaire* (Paris: Presses Universitaires de France, 1965); and also from the same perspective, H. Frei, *La Grammaire des fautes* (Paris, 1929; Geneva: Slatkine Reprints, 1971).

5. See J. Cellard and A. Rey, *Dictionnaire du français non conventionel* (Paris: Hachette, 1980), viii.

6. Let it suffice to note, for example, that in the discourse gathered on the least strained market—a conversation between women—the lexicon of slang is almost totally absent; in the case observed, it only appears when one of the speakers quotes the words of a man (*"tu va m'fout' le camp tout d'suite"*) to which she immediately adds, "That's how he talks, like an old Parisian kid, yeah, he has a kind of hard luck look, his cap always to one side, oh yeah, you can see!" A little later the same character repeats the word *"pognon"*—slang for money, "dough"— right after having related the words of a café owner in which it appeared. See Y. Delsaut, "L'économie du langage populaire," *Actes de la Recherche en Sciences Sociales* 4 (July 1975): 33–40. Empirical analysis ought to attempt to determine the speakers' feelings about a word belonging to slang or legitimate language (instead of imposing the observer's definition); among other things, that would allow us to understand numerous traits described as "errors" that are the product of a misplaced sense of distinction.

7. That is what makes the legitimate language, in the guise of going in circles or nowhere, so often turn to the advantage of the dominants, like so many circular definitions or tautologies of vulgarity and distinction.

8. Given the role played by spontaneous sociolinguistics and express interventions by families and schools that they prompt and direct in the maintenance or the transformation of the language, a sociolinguistic analysis of linguistic change cannot ignore this sort of *linguistic custom* or *right* that in particular determines pedagogical practices.

9. Even as he accepts the division that is fundamental to the very notion of "popular language," Henri Bauche observes that the "bourgeois speech in its familiar use presents numerous traits in common with popular language" (Bauche, *Langage populaire*, 9). And later, "The boundaries between slang—the various slangs—and popular language are sometimes

difficult to determine. Quite vague as well are the lines between popular language and familiar language, first, and second, between popular language strictly speaking and the language of the common folk, those who, without being precisely of the people, lack instruction or education, those whom the 'bourgeois' characterize as 'common'" (26).

10. Even though, for complex reasons that need to be examined, the dominant vision does not give it a central place, the opposition between masculine and feminine is one of the principles beginning from which are engendered the oppositions most typical of the "people" as a "female" populace, changeable and hungry for sensual pleasure (according to the antithesis of head/womb).

11. This is what makes praising the speech of the "real real men" ambiguous: the vision of the world that is expressed by it and the virile virtues of the *durs de durs* find their natural extension in what has been called the "popular right" (see Z. Sternhell, *La Droite révolutionnaire, 1885–1914: Les origines du fascisme* [Paris: Le Seuil, 1978]), a fascist-like combination of racism, nationalism, and authoritarianism. And we can better comprehend the obvious bizarrerie represented by the case of Céline.

12. Everything seems to indicate that with the prolonging of schooling, the "tough" character is now formed as early as school age, and in opposition to all forms of submission that school requires.

13. It is one of the effects of class racism, according to which all the "poor," like Asians or blacks, resemble one another, that it leads to the unconscious exclusion of the very possibility of a difference (of tact, invention, competence, and so on) and a pursuit of the difference. The undifferentiated praise of the "popular" that characterizes populism can thus lead to exulting confidently over demonstrations that "natives" consider inept, idiotic, or crude, or, what amounts to the same thing, it can lead to retaining of the "common" only what is out of the ordinary, and considering it representative of ordinary speech.

14. The young "toughs" coming from immigrant families clearly represent the outer limit of the revolt of adolescents coming from economically and culturally deprived families, which is often based in difficulties,

disappointments, or failures in school, as far as it can be pushed toward the total rejection of "French" society, symbolized by school and also by routine racism.

15. P. E. Willis, *Profane Culture* (London: Routledge & Kegan Paul, 1978), see esp. 48–50.

16. As an exemplary demonstration of this principle of classification and of the vastness of its field of application, it suffices to cite the builder (a former miner) who, when asked to categorize the names of professions (in a test conceived on the model of the techniques used for the componential analysis of terms of kinship) and to give a name to the categories thus produced, dismissed with a hand gesture a cluster of higher professions, the paradigm of which was for him the television show host, saying, "all the *pédés*—queers" (Yvette Delsaut Study, Denain, 1978).

17. In a more general fashion, because the more or less blunt evocation of sexual matters and the flattening projection of the sentimental onto the physiological level often have the value of *euphemisms through hyperbole or antiphrasis*, which, opposite of understatement, say more in order to say less, this lexicon changes meaning completely when it changes markets, with novelistic transcription or lexicological recollection.

18. The equivalent of this situation might only be encountered in the form of military service, which was no doubt one of the principal places for the production and inculcation of forms of slang speech.

19. The small business owner, and especially the bar owner, particularly when he possesses the virtues of sociability that are part of professional requirements, is never the object of statutory hostility on the part of workers (contrary to what intellectuals and members of the petite bourgeoisie with cultural capital tend to assume, who are separated from them by a true cultural barrier). He very often enjoys a certain symbolic authority—which can be exercised even on the political plane, even if the subject is tacitly taboo in café conversation—because of the ease and assurance that he owes among other things to his economic ease.

20. It should be ascertained whether, in addition to bar owners, merchants, and in particular professionals in sales talk and patter like street vendors

and the hawkers at markets or fairs, as well butchers and in a different style, corresponding to different structures of interaction, hairdressers and barbers don't contribute more to the production of coinages than the workers who are simple *occasional* producers.

21. This representation assigns to the masculine a social nature—that of the "tough" man and "tireless worker," "of few words," rejecting feelings and sentimentality, solid and "all of a piece," honest and dependable, "a man you can count on," and so on—that the harshness of living conditions would impose on him in any case but that he feels it is his duty to choose because it defines itself in opposition to the "feminine" nature (and to the effeminate "counternature"): weak, gentle, docile, submissive, fragile, changeable, sensitive, sensual. This principle of division acts not only in its specific field of application, that is to say, in the domain of the relationships between the sexes, but in a very broad way by imposing on men a strict, rigid—in a word, essentialist—vision of their identity and more generally of other social identities, and thus of the whole social order.

22. It goes without saying that these behaviors tend to vary according to the woman's level of education and especially according to the difference in educational levels between spouses.

23. It is clear that according to this logic, women are always at fault; that is to say, it is in their (faulty) nature. The examples could be multiplied to infinity: in the case where the woman is appointed to take the necessary steps, if she succeeds, it is because it was easy; if she fails, it is because she didn't know how to do it.

24. The intention of inflicting a symbolic stain (through insult, gossip, or erotic provocation, for example) on what is perceived as inaccessible contains the most terrible admission of recognizing superiority. So it is that, as Jean Starobinski has clearly shown, "crude talk, far from closing the distance between social ranks, maintains and increases it; under the guise of irreverence and freedom, it abounds in the sense of degradation, it is the self-confirmation of inferiority." (This concerns the servants' gossip regarding Mademoiselle de Breil—see J.-J. Rousseau,

Confessions III in *Oeuvres complètes* [Paris: Gallimard, 1959], 94–96, as analyzed by Starobinski in *La Relation critique* [Paris: Gallimard, 1970], 98–154.)

3. "We, the People": Thoughts on Freedom of Assembly

Parts of this discussion are drawn from Judith Butler, *Notes Toward a Performative Theory of Assembly* (Cambridge, Mass.: Harvard University Press, 2015).

1. H. Arendt, *The Human Condition*. (Chicago: University of Chicago Press, 1958).

2. United Nations, "Universal Declaration of Human Rights" (1948), articles 20, 23.

3. The International Labour Organization makes clear that the right to freedom of peaceable assembly is central to collective bargaining and participation and membership in international labor organizations. See D. Tajgman and K. Curtis, *Freedom of Association: A User's Guide, Standards, Principles, and Procedures of the International Labour Organization* (Geneva: International Labour Information, 2000), 6.

4. See my "Performativity's Social Magic," in *Bourdieu: A Critical Reader*, ed. R. Shusterman (London: Basil Blackwell, 1999).

5. J. L. Austin, *How to Do Things with Words*, ed. J. O. Urmson and M. Sbisa (Cambridge, Mass.: Harvard University Press, 1962), lecture 9.

6. See J. Derrida, "Declarations of Independence," trans. T. Keenan and T. Pepper, *New Political Science* 15 (Summer 1986): 3–19. See also M. Canovan, *The People* (Cambridge: Polity, 2005); E. Balibar, *We, the People of Europe? Reflections on Transnational Citizenship*, trans. J. Swenson (Princeton: Princeton University Press, 2004); and J. Frank, *Constituent Moments: Enacting the People in Postrevolutionary America* (Durham, N.C.: Duke University Press, 2010).

7. S. Felman, *Le scandale du corps parlant* (Paris: Seuil, 1980), republished as *The Scandal of the Speaking Body* (Stanford, Calif.: Stanford University Press, 2002). Some of my remarks offered in the introduction to that text are reworked in this text.

8. See E. Laclau, *On Populist Reason* (London: Verso, 2005) for a different account of demands and their propositional forms.

9. H. Arendt, *The Human Condition* (Chicago: University of Chicago Press, 1958), 199.

10. See my "Introduction: Precarious Life, Grievable Life," in *Frames of War: When Is Life Grievable?* (London: Verso, 2009).

11. See Donna Haraway's views on complex relationalities in *Simians, Cyborgs, and Women* (New York: Routledge, 1991) and *The Companion Species Manifesto* (Chicago: Prickly Paradigm Press, 2003).

4. To Render Sensible

1. H. Arendt, *Qu'est-ce que la politique?* (1950–1959), trans. S. Courtine-Denamy (Paris: Le Seuil, 1995), 39–43. [Trans.:—See Arendt, *The Promise of Politics*, ed. J. Kohn, trans. J. Woods (New York: Random House, 2005).]

2. *First Contact*, directed by B. Connolly and R. Anderson (New York: Filmmakers Library, 1982). See F. Niney, *L'Épreuve du réel à l'écran: Essai sur le principe de réalité documentaire* (Brussels: De Boeck Université, 2000), 283.

3. I have already tried to justify this plural in *Peuples exposés, peuples figurants*, L'oeil de l'histoire 4 (Paris: Les Éditions de Minuit, 2012).

4. See "Populisms," special issue, *Critique* 68, no. 776–77 (2012).

5. P. Rosanvallon, *Le Peuple introuvable: Histoire de la représentation démocratique en France* (Paris: Gallimard, 1998), 11, 13, with a reference to the article by O. Beaud, "*Repräsentation* et *Stellvertretung*: Sur une distinction de Carl Schmitt," *Droits: Revue française de théorie juridique*, no. 6 (1987): 11–20.

6. C. Schmitt, *Theorie de la Constitution* (1928), trans. L. Deroche (Paris: Presses Universitaires de France, 1993), 347 (translation slightly modified). [Trans.:—See Schmitt, *Constitutional Theory*, J. Seitzer (Durham, N.C.: Duke University Press, 2008).]

7. Ibid., 218, 381, 419–20, and so on. See also C. Schmitt, *État, mouvement, peuple: L'organisation triadique de l'unité politique* (1933), trans. A. Pilleul (Paris: Éditions Kimé, 1997), 48–63. [Trans.:—See Schmitt, *State, Movement, People*, trans. S. Draghici (Corvallis, Ore.: Plutarch Press, 2001).] I have

discussed the use of these Carl Schmitt texts by Giorgio Agamben (in *Le Règne et la gloire: Pour une généologie théologique de l'économie et du gouvernement [Homo sacer II, 2]* [2007], trans. J. Gayraud and M. Rueff [Paris: Le Seuil, 2008]) in *Survivance des lucioles* (Paris: Les Éditions de Minuit, 2009), 77–97.

8. See C. Schmitt, *Parlementarism et démocratie* (1924–1931), trans. J.-L. Schlegel (Paris: Le Seuil, 1988). [Trans.:—See Schmitt, *The Crisis of Parlimentary Democracy*, trans. E. Kennedy (Cambridge, Mass.: MIT Press, 1998).]

9. Rosanvallon, *Le Peuple introuvable*, 440–41, 445–46, 447–48.

10. Ibid., 447.

11. For "syncopes," see L. Marin, "Ruptures, interruptions, syncopes dans la représentation de peinture" (1992), in *De la représentation*, ed. D. Arasse, A. Cantillon, G. Careri, D. Cohn, P.-A. Fabre, and F. Marin (Paris: Le Seuil-Gallimard, 1994), 364–76. For "rips," see G. Didi-Huberman, *Devant l'image: Question posée aux fins d'une histoire de l'art* (Paris: Les Éditions de Minuit, 1990), 169–269 ("L'image comme déchirure"). [Trans.:—See Didi-Huberman, *Confronting Images: Questioning the Ends of a Certain History of Art*, trans. J. Goodman (University Park: Penn State University Press, 2005).]

12. See G. Didi-Huberman, *Devant le temps: Histoire de l'art et anachronisme des images* (Paris: Les Éditions de Minuit, 2000). Also see the recent issue of the online journal *Trivium* no. 10 (2012), edited by M. Pic and E. Alloa.

13. See G. Didi-Huberman, *L'Image survivante: Histoire de l'art et temps des fantômes selon Aby Warburg* (Paris: Les Éditions de Minuit, 2002), 115–270.

14. S. Freud, *L'Interprétation du rêve* (1900), trans. J. Altounian, P. Cotet, R. Lainé, A. Rauzy, and F. Robert (2003; repr., Paris: Presses Universitaires de France, 2010), 509–11. [Trans.:—See Freud, *The Interpretation of Dreams*, trans. J. Strachey (New York: Basic Books, 1955).]

15. W. Benjamin, *Paris, capitale du XIXᵉ siècle: Le Livre des passages* (1927–1940), trans. J. Lacoste (Paris: Éditions de Cerf, 1989), 481n4.1. [Trans.:—See Benjamin, *The Arcades Project*, trans. H. Eiland and K. McLaughlin (Cambridge, Mass.: Harvard University Press, 2002).]

16. W. Benjamin, "L'oeuvre d'art à l'ère de sa reproductibilité technique" (first version, 1935), trans. R. Rochlitz, *Oeuvres III* (Paris: Gallimard, 2000), 93–94. [Trans.:—See Benjamin, *Illuminations*, trans. H. Zohn (New York: Random House, 1968).]

17. W. Benjamin, "Sur le concept d'histoire" (1940), trans. M. de Gandillac revised by P. Rusch, in *Oeuvres III*, 430. [Trans.:—See Benjamin, *Illuminations*.]

18. Ibid., 440–41.

19. Ibid., 431.

20. Ibid., 433.

21. W. Benjamin, "Paralipomènes et variantes des 'Thèses sur le concept d'histoire'" (1940), trans. J.-M. Monnoyer, in *Écrits français* (Paris: Gallimard, 1991), 346.

22. Benjamin, "Sur le concept d'histoire," 441.

23. See S. Freud, *Métapsychologie* (1915), trans. J. Laplanche and J.-B. Pontalis (Paris: Gallimard, 1968), 45–63. [Trans.:—See Freud, *On Metapsychology*, trans. J. Strachey (New York: Penguin Books, 1991).]

24. See H. Arendt, *La Tradition cachée: Le Juif comme paria* (1944–1948), trans. S. Courtine-Demany (1987; repr., Paris: Christian Bourgois, 1997). [Trans.:—See Arendt, *The Jew as Pariah*, ed. R. Feldman (New York: Grove Press, 1978).]

25. M. de Certeau, *La Solitude, une vérité oubliée de la communication* (with F. Roustang et al.) (Paris: Desclée de Brouwer, 1967); *L'Absent de l'histoire* (Tours: Mame, 1973); *L'Invention du quotidien* (Paris: Union générale d'Éditions, 1980; Paris: Gallimard, 1990–1994). [Trans.:—See Certeau, *The Practice of Everyday Life*, trans. S. Rendall (Berkeley: University of California Press, 1984).]

26. M. Foucault, *Folie et déraison: Histoire de la folie à l'âge classique* (Paris: Plon, 1961; Paris: Gallimard, 1972); *Naissance de la clinique: Une archéologie du regard médical* (Paris: Presses Universitaires de France, 1963); *Raymond Roussel* (Paris: Gallimard, 1963); *Surveiller et punir: Naissance de la prison* (Paris: Gallimard, 1975); *Histoire de la sexualité* (Paris: Gallimard, 1976–1994).

27. M. Foucault, "Espace, savoir et pouvoir" (1982), in *Dits et écrits 1954–1988, IV: 1980–1988*, ed. D. Defert, F. Ewald, and J. Lagrange (Paris: Gallimard, 1994), 273–77.

28. Foucault, "Des espaces autres" (1984), in *Dits et écrits*, 756, 758–59, 762.

29. A. Farge, *Le Goût de l'archive* (Paris: Le Seuil, 1989). [Trans.:—See Farge, *The Allure of the Archives*, trans. T. Scott-Railton (New Haven, Conn.: Yale University Press, 2013).]

30. A. Warburg, "L'art du portrait et la bourgeoissie florentine: Domenico Ghirlandaio à Santa Trinita: Les portraits de Laurent de Médicis et de son entourage" (1902), trans. S. Muller, in *Essais florentins* (Paris: Klincksieck, 1990), 106. [Trans.:—See Warburg, "The Art of Portraiture and the Florentine Bourgeoisie," in *The Renewal of Pagan Antiquity*, trans. D. Britt (Los Angeles: Getty Research Institute for the History of Art and the Humanities, 1999).]

31. A. Farge, *Le Vol d'aliments à Paris au XVIIIe siècle: délinquance et criminalité* (Paris: Plon, 1974).

32. A. Farge, *Dire et mal dire: l'opinion publique au XVIIIe siècle* (Paris: Le Seuil, 1992); *Le Bracelet et le parchemin: l'écrit sur soi au XVIIIe siècle* (Paris: Bayard, 2003); "Walter Benjamin et le dérangement des habitudes historiennes," in "Walter Benjamin: la tradition des vaincus," special issue, *Cahiers d'anthropologie sociale*, no. 4 (2008) 27–32.

33. A. Farge, *Vivre dans la rue à Paris au VXIIIe siècle* (Paris: Gallimard-Julliard, 1979; Paris: Gallimard, 1992); (with M. Foucault), *Le Désordre des familles: Lettres de cachet des archives de la Bastille au XVIIIe siècle* (Paris: Gallimard-Julliard, 1982); *La Vie fragile: Violence, pouvoirs et solidartés à Paris au XVIIIe siècles* (Paris: Hachette, 1986; Paris: Le Seuil, 1992). [Trans.:—See A. Farge and C. Shelton, *Fragile Lives: Violence, Power, and Solidarity in Eighteenth-Century Paris* (Cambridge, Mass.: Harvard University Press, 1993).]

34. A. Farge, *Effusion et tourment, le récit des corps: Histoire du peuple au XVIIIe siècle* (Paris: Odile Jacob, 2007), 9–10. See more recently, *Essai pour une histoire des voix au dix-huitième siècle* (Paris: Bayard, 2009). A continuation of these problematics is found in the work collected by the Maurice

Florence Collective, *Archives de l'infamie* (Paris: Les Prairies ordinaire, 2009).

35. Arlette Farge refers here to the book by D. Le Breton, *Les Passions ordinaires: Anthropologie des émotions* (Paris: Armand Colin-Massion, 1998; Paris: Payot & Rivages, 2004).

36. A. Faure and J. Rancière, *La Parole ouvrière* (Paris: Union générale d'Éditions, 1976; Paris: La Fabrique, 2007); J. Rancière, *La Nuit des prolétaires: Archives du rêve ouvrier* (Paris: Fayard, 1981; Paris: Hachette Litteeratures, 2009). See also *Les Scènes du peuple (Les Révoltes logiques, 1975–1985)* (Lyons: Horlieu Éditions, 2003). [Trans.:—See Rancière, *Proletariat Nights: The Workers' Dream in the Nineteenth Century*, trans. J. Drury (London: Verso, 2012); *Staging the People: The Proletariat and His Double*, trans. D. Fernbach (London: Verso, 2011).]

37. See É. Zola, *Carnets d'enquêtes: Une ethnographie inédité de la France (1871–1890)*, ed. H. Mitterand (Paris: Plon, 1986); J. Rancière, *Courts Voyages au pays du peuple* (Paris: Le Seuil, 1990), 89–135. [Trans.:—See Rancière, *Short Voyages to the Land of the People*, trans. J. Swenson (Stanford, Calif.: Stanford University Press, 2003).]

38. Benjamin, *Paris, capital du XIXe siècle*, 481.

39. See C. Lefort, "La politique et la pensée de la politique" (1963), in *Sur une colonne absent: Écrits autour de Merleau-Ponty* (Paris: Gallimard, 1978), 45–104; *Les Formes de l'histoire: Essais d'anthropologie politique* (1978; repr., Paris: Gallimard, 2000); and *Essais sur le politique, XIXe–XXe siècles* (1986; repr., Paris: Le Seuil, 2001).

40. See M. Merleau-Ponty, *Les Aventures de la dialectique* (1955; repr., Paris: Gallimard, 2000), 17–45 ("La crise de l'entendement"); "Partout et nulle part" (1956), in *Signes* (Paris: Gallimard, 1960), 194–200 ("Existence et dialectique"); *Le Visible et l'invisible (1959–1961)*, ed. C. Lefort (1964; repr., Paris: Gallimard, 1983), 75–141 ("Interrogation et dialectique"). For a recent philosophic rehabilitation of the sensible, see the fine book by E. Coccia, *La Vie sensible*, trans. M. Reuff (Paris: Payot & Rivages, 2010). [Trans.:—See Merleau-Ponty, *Adventures in the Dialectic*, trans. J. Bien (Evanston, Ill.: Northwestern University Press, 1973); *Signs*, trans. R.

McCleary (Evanston, Ill.: Northwestern University Press, 1964); and *The Visible and the Invisible*, trans. A. Lingis (Evanston, Ill.: Northwestern University Press, 1968).]

41. J. Rancière, *Le Partage du sensible: Esthétique et politique* (Paris: La Fabrique, 2000). [Trans.:—See Rancière, *Dissensus: On Politics and Aesthetics*, trans. S. Corcoran (New York: Continuum, 2010).]

42. J. Rancière, *Aux bords du politique* (Paris: La Fabrique, 1998; Paris: Galllimard, 2004), 242, 244. [Trans.:—See Rancière, *On the Shores of Politics*, trans. L. Heron (London: Verso, 2007).]

43. A. Badiou, "La politique: Une dialectique non expressive" (2005), in *La Relation énigmatique entre philosophie et politique* (Meaux: Éditions Germina, 2011), 70–71.

44. J. Rancière, *Le Philosophe et ses pauvres* (Paris: Fayard, 1983; Paris: Flammarion, 2007), vi (2006 preface). [Trans.:—See Rancière, *The Philosopher and His Poor*, trans. A. Parker, J. Drury, and C. Oster (Durham, N.C.: Duke University Press, 2004).]

45. M. Merleau-Ponty, "Le roman de la métaphysique" (1945), in *Sens et non-sens* (Paris: Éditions Nagel, 1948; Paris: Gallimard, 1996), 35–37. [Trans.:—See Merleau-Ponty, *Sense and Non-Sense*, trans. H. and P. A. Dreyfus (Evanston, Ill.: Northwestern University Press, 1964).]

46. J. Rancière, *Aisthesis: Scènes du régime esthétique de l'art* (Paris: Éditions Galilée, 2011). [Trans.:—See Rancière, *Aiethesis: Scenes from the Aesthetic Regime of Art*, trans. Z. Paul (London: Verso, 2013).]

47. Ibid., 287–307. See J. Agee and W. Evans, *Louons maintenant les grands hommes: Alabama, trois familles de métayers en 1936* (1941), trans. J. Queval (1977; repr., Paris: Plon, 2002). [Trans.:—See Agee and Evans, *Now Let Us Praise Famous Men* (New York: Houghton Mifflin, 1941).]

48. See V. Maïakovski, *L'Universel Reportage (1913–1929)*, trans. H. Deluy (Tours: Farrago, 2001).

49. See esp. C. Reznikoff, *Témoignage: Les États-Unis (1885–1915), recitatif* (1965), trans. M. Cholodenko (Paris: P.O.L., 2012); W. G. Sebald, *Austerlitz* (2001), trans. P. Charbonneau (Arles: Actes Sud, 2002); and J.-C. Bailly, *Le Dépaysement: Voyages en France* (Paris: Le Seuil, 2011). See

the studies of M. Pic, "Du montage de témoignages dans le littérature: Holocauste de Charles Reznikoff," *Critique*, no. 736 (2008): 878–88; "Élégies documentaires," *Europe* no. 1033 (2012): *****. [Trans.:—See Reznikoff, *Testimony: The United States (1885–1915) Recitative* (New York: New Directions, 1965); Sebald, *Austerlitz*, trans. A. Bell (New York: Random House, 2001).]

50. See G. Didi-Huberman, *Atlas ou le gai savoir inquiet*, L'oeil de l'histoire 3 (Paris: Les Éditions de Minuit, 2011).

51. B. Cendrars, *Kodak (documentaire)* (Paris: Stock, 1924); *Poésies complètes* (Paris: Denoël, 1944), 151–89 ("Documentaires"). [Trans.:—See *Blaise Cendrars: Complete Poems*, trans. R. Padgett (Berkeley: University of California Press, 1992).] See D. Grojnowski, *Photographie et langage: Fictions, illustrations, informations, visions, théories* (Paris: Librairie José Corti, 2002), 45–66.

52. A. Breton, *Nadja* (1928), *Oeuvres complètes 1*, ed. M. Bonnet (Paris: Gallimard, 1988), 643–753. [Trans.:—See Breton, *Nadja*, trans. R. Howard (New York: Grove Press, 1960).]

53. See G. Didi-Huberman, *La Ressemblance inform, or le gai savoir visuel selon Georges Bataille* (Paris: Macula, 1995).

54. See U. Marx, G. Schwarz, M. Schwarz, and E. Wizisla, *Walter Benjamin: Archives; images, textes et signes* (2006), ed. F. Perrier, trans. P. Ivernel (Paris: Klincksieck, 2011), 272–93.

55. I. Ehrenbourg, *[Mon Paris]* (Moscow: Izogiz, 1933; Paris: Éditions 7L, 2005).

56. See O. Lugon, *Le Style documentaire: d'August Sander à Walker Evans, 1920–1945* (2001; repr., Paris: Macula, 2011). G. Didi-Huberman, *Quand les images prennent position*, L'oeil de l'histoire 1 (Paris, Les Éditions de Minuit, 2009).

57. Agee and Evans, *Now Let Us Praise*, unpaginated photos.

58. M. Blanchot, *La Communauté inavouable* (Paris: Les Éditions de Minuit, 1983), 54. [Trans.:—See Blanchot, *The Unavowable Community*, trans. P. Jorris (Barrytown, N.Y.: Station Hill Books, 2006).]

59. I have altered Maurice Blanchot's expression in the French here because of the distinction, which seems to me necessary (one will find it, notably, in the commentaries on Nietzsche by Gilles Deleuze), between *puissance*

(power, strength) and *pouvoir* (power, ability). Thus one could say that a "declaration of powerlessness" (inability) is not exactly deprived of its power (strength) of declaration.

5. The People and the Third People

1. It seems to me that it can be claimed that in American democracy the citizenship is especially individualized whereas in the French republic it is more collective, identified with popular sovereignty.

2. I have attempted to back up this hypothesis in *La Contre-révolution coloniale en France: De de Gaulle à Sarkozy* (Paris: La Fabrique, 2009).

3. See notably J.-L. Mélanchon, "Une défense souveraine et altermondialiste," *Revue Défense nationale*, no. 749 (April 2012).

4. F.-B. Éwanjé-Épée and S. Magliani-Belkacem, "Les luttes d'immigration postcoloniale dans la 'révolution citoyenne,'" *Contretemps*, September 6, 2012, http://www.contretemps.eu/interventions/luttes-immigration-postcoloniale-dans-«révolution-citoyenne». The declarations of Jean-Luc Mélanchon also prompted excellent reaction from a few militants of the Left Front, members of one of the movements stemming from the anticapitalist New Party: C. Durand, R. Keucheyan, J. Rivoire, and F. Verri, "Jean-Luc Mélanchon, vous avez tort sur les émueutes d'Amiens-Nord," *Rue89*, August 31, 2012, http://rue89.nouvelobs.com/rue89-politique/2012/08/31/jean-luc-melenchon-vous-avez-tort-sur-les-emeutes-damiens-nord-234968.

5. Malcolm X, *Le Pouvoir noir*, ed. G. Breitman, trans. G. Carle (Paris: La Découverte, 2008), 208. [Trans.:—See *By Any Means Necessary: Malcolm X Speeches and Writings* (New York: Pathfinder, 1970).]

6. These questions are approached in my latest essay, *Malcolm X: Stratège de la dignité noire* (Paris: Amsterdam, 2013).

7. See S. Khiari, "Nous avons besoin d'une stratégie décoloniale," in *Races et capitalisme*, ed. F. Boggio Éwanjé-Épée and S. Magliani-Belkacem (Paris: Syllepse, 2012).

8. I began to consider this question in *Pour une politique de la racialle* (Paris: Textuel, 2006).

6. The Populism That Is Not to Be Found

This chapter originally appeared in *Libération* (January 3, 2011) and has been revised for the present volume.

Conclusion: Fragile Collectivities, Imagined Sovereignties

1. A. Badiou, "Twenty-Four Notes on the Uses of the Word 'People,'" in this volume, 28.

2. Ibid., 22–24.

3. Ibid., 30–31.

4. P. Bourdieu, *Distinction: A Social Critique of the Judgement of Taste*, trans. R.Nice (Cambridge, Mass.: Harvard University Press, 1984), 99–168.

5. G.-F. Coyer, *Dissertation sur la nature du peuple*, in *Bagatelles morales et dissertations par Mr. L'Abbé Coyer; avec le testament litteraire de Mr. L'Abbé Desfontaines* ([Frankfurt?]: Knoch & Eslinger, 1757), British Library, 225–26.

6. Voltaire to Damilaville, April 1, 1766 (D13232), in *The Complete Works of Voltaire*, vol. 114: *Correspondence,* ed. T. Besterman (Banbury, UK: Voltaire Foundation, 1973), 155–56.

7. Coyer, *Dissertation*, 232–34.

8. Bourdieu, *Distinction*, 397–465; "You Said 'Popular,'" in this volume, 46–47.

9. J. Butler, "'We, the People': Thoughts on Freedom of Assembly," in this volume, 50.

10. Ibid., 51.

11. E. Laclau, *On Populist Reason* (London: Verso, 2005); J. Habermas, *Between Facts and Norms: Contributions to a Discourse Theory of Law and Democracy*, trans. W. Rehg (Cambridge, Mass.: MIT Press, 1996), 329–87.

12. J. Butler, *Excitable Speech: A Politics of the Performative* (New York: Routledge, 1997), 12, 15–16, 77–79; W. Benjamin, "Critique of Violence," in *Selected Writings, Volume 1, 1913–1926*, trans. E. Jephcott (Cambridge, Mass.: Harvard University Press, 1996); J. Derrida, *The Beast and the Sovereign, Volume 1*, trans. G. Bennington (Chicago: University of Chicago Press, 2009); M. Foucault, *"Society Must Be Defended": Lectures at the Collège de France 1975–1976*, trans. D. Macey (New York: Picador, 2003), 36–40, 43–44; Carl

Schmitt, *Political Theology: Four Chapters on the Concept of Sovereignty*, trans. G. Schwab (Chicago: University of Chicago Press, 1985).

13. Butler, *Excitable Speech*, 77–78.

14. Butler, "We, the People,"53.

15. G. Didi-Huberman, *Peuples exposés, Peuples figurants* (Paris: Les Éditions de Minuit, 2012), 17; "To Render Sensible," in this volume, 84.

16. Didi-Huberman, "To Render Sensible,"74–78.

17. Ibid., 85.

18. Didi-Huberman, *Peuples exposés*, 96–105.

19. Ibid., 33, 108–9.

20. Ibid., 105.

21. Ibid., 30–31.

22. J. Rancière, "The Populism That Is Not to Be Found," in this volume, 105.

23. Collected and translated as J. Rancière, *Staging the People: The Proletarian and His Double*, trans. D. Fernbach (London: Verso, 2011) and *The Intellectual and His People: Staging the People, Volume 2*, trans. D. Fernbach (London: Verso, 2012).

24. I have developed this narrative in greater detail in *Imagined Sovereignties: The Power of the People and Other Myths of the Modern Age* (New York: Cambridge University Press, 2016).

25. H. Arendt, *On Revolution* (New York: Penguin, 2006), 248–50.

26. Olson, *Imagined Sovereignties*, chap. 4.

27. S. Khiari, "The People and the Third People," in this volume, 87–88, 89.

28. Olson, *Imagined Sovereignties*, chap. 5.

29. B. Anderson, *Imagined Communities: Reflections on the Origin and Spread of Nationalism*, rev. ed. (London: Verso, 1991), 178–85; R. Smith, *Stories of Peoplehood: The Politics and Morals of Political Membership* (Cambridge: Cambridge University Press, 2003), 64–69, 103–16.

30. E. Sieyès, "What Is the Third Estate?" (1789), in *Political Writings*, ed. and trans. M. Sonenscher (Indianapolis: Hackett, 2003), 136.

31. J. Derrida, "Declarations of Independence," trans. T. Keenan and T. Pepper, *New Political Science* 7, no. 1 (1986): 10; Derrida, *The Politics of*

Friendship, trans. G. Collins (London: Verso, 2005), 306; J. Frank, *Constituent Moments: Enacting the People in Postrevolutionary America* (Durham, N.C.: Duke University Press, 2010), 5–6.

32. Derrida, "Declarations of Independence," 10; Frank, *Constituent Moments*, 8; B. Honig, "Declarations of Independence: Arendt and Derrida on the Problem of Founding a Republic," *American Political Science Review* 85, no. 1 (1991): 97–113.

INDEX

people (*continued*)
noun, 21; as not existing, 66, 102; as not to be found, 70; the people's people, 28; as political category, 1, 3, 4, 13, 20, 31; as political collectivity with special normative status, 120; as political notion, 89; positive senses of term, 30–31; as privileged term for articulating sphere of modern politics, 2–3; racial dimension of notion of, 90; as rendered sensible, 80–86, 117, 118, 119, 120, 122, 131; as result of process of political becoming, 5; revalorization of category of, 15; social ontology of, 121; and socioeconomic order, 90; as standing for new forms of decentralized, democratized epistemology, 125; strategic dimension of, 89; as taking on normative value, 129; talking about in the plural, 2; as term of art in ancien régime, 125; use of term when accompanied by an adjective, 22, 23–24; virtualization of in contemporary politics, 114. *See also specific groups of people*
people-nation, 89, 90
peoples, as having powers, 131

performative enactments, 53, 54–55, 58, 113, 114
performativity, 108, 112–17, 122, 129, 130
permanent revolution, 115
Plato, 19, 29, 69, 80, 84
plural action, 52, 55
plural body/plural bodies, 60, 63
plurality: of bodies, 59, 61; condition of, 58
political action: background assumptions about, 123; collective political action, 112, 113; crux of, 14
political becoming, process of, 5
political depoliticization and exclusion, 111
political effectiveness of relics, 72
political imaginaries, 108, 120, 122, 130
political plurality, 63
political sociality, 56
political sovereignty, 116
Political Theology (Schmitt), 67
political theory, role/text of, 3, 4
politics: communist politics, 31, 109; final aim of, 62; of power, 95; progressive politics, 30; of the street, 59, 113; survival as precondition of, 60; of the truth, 80
popular, 4, 22, 25, 32–48, 109–10; art, 33, 35; classes, 33–35;

NEW DIRECTIONS IN CRITICAL THEORY

Amy Allen, General Editor